M000169864

UNCOVER
THE HIDDEN
JOB MARKET

How to find and
win your next
Senior Executive role

TESTIMONIALS

"Richard Triggs is one of the leading authorities in Australia for executive leaders wanting to fast-track their careers to C-Suite and board positions. I congratulate him on behalf of all in the Australian Institute of Management." – *Grant Dearlove, Chair, Australian Institute of Management*

"It is very rare that an industry leader can identify disruptive innovations in their field. It is even rarer that they can respond effectively. Richard Triggs has done both, and distilled this wisdom into a simple, no-nonsense guide. This book is a 'must read' for any senior executive who wants to find and capture the right opportunities in a rapidly changing employment market." – *Martin Moore, CEO, CS Energy*

"If you are looking for someone to keep you actively engaged, hanging onto every word, and smiling at the same time then Richard is your man! I got so much out of the 'Always Stand Out Workshop' that I have recommended it to many of my colleagues because I wanted them to have the same learning experience that I had. Life is all about continued learning and sharing and this workshop has it all. I walked out of that room invigorated and excited about what I could do to reinvent myself so that I will 'Always Stand Out'." – *Shirley Robertson, Former Chief Operating Officer, Queensland Motorways*

"I would consider Richard to be Australia's best advisor when it comes to accelerating your executive and board career, and give him my highest recommendation. I have witnessed first hand the results of Richard's industry-leading approach." – *Vivienne Anthon, former CEO, Australian Institute of Management*

"If you are a senior executive, CEO or Board Member wanting to take your career to the next level and work for Australia's leading companies, then Richard Triggs is the advisor to engage. Not only will he give you all of the inside information required into the corporate sector, but he also has an exceptional reputation amongst the top level corporate senior executive." – *Tim Dwyer, CEO, Shirlaws Australia*

"I highly recommend Richard Triggs if you want advice and coaching to gain strong momentum to further your C-suite or board career. He has a cutting-edge approach, and gets to the core of what's needed quickly." – *Fulton Smith, Managing Director, Gravitas Leadership Group*

"Richard is highly regarded in corporate circles as Australia's leading consultant in executive career management. His intimate knowledge of the executive job market, coupled with his access to the hidden executive job market place makes him a stand out." – *Glen Carlson, Global CEO, Key Person of Influence (KPI) Programme*

"I recently attended one of Richard's 'Always Stand Out' workshops. Very well prepared and presented, the workshop provides a welcome boost and reflects Richard's experience and empathy as an executive coach. Highly recommended, particularly in the current climate." – *Ross Muller, Principal, AChord Management*

"Always Stand Out is a fantastic course. I learnt more in 2 hours from Richard than I have heard over the last 18 months from executive search specialists. A definite course to attend for those seeking insight about the hidden job market." – *Ashley Busse, Senior Executive Director, Department of Premier and Cabinet*

"I would like to take this opportunity to thank you for a fantastic Webinar yesterday – 'Always Stand Out – Executive Job Search Workshop'. The information covered was exactly what I was looking for and I was left feeling empowered and motivated. Richard's knowledge of the recruitment industry and the tools available to both employers and employees is second to none. By following the simple steps suggested by Richard, executives can take control of their LinkedIn profiles and strategically plan their next career position using their individual brand and online presence to maximum potential." – *Tanya Henry, Teacher, TAFE Queensland*

"The Always Stand Out presentation was worth the investment; it was very insightful and contained great tips on how to improve my profile and chances of gaining my preferred role." – *Simon Parker, Director, Sporting Industry*

"I signed up for the presentation with mixed feelings as to the relevance for my pending career change. I was, however, totally 'blown away' with the quality, relevance and content of the presentation. Richard is able to combine an engaging and relaxed style with an ability to cover

a large range of relevant detail. The keyword here is relevant. If you are considering a career change I cannot think of a better use of your time than attending this 150-minute presentation. You WILL save untold hours of wasted time in your search to find your next career challenge."
– *Simon Jeffrey, Former CEO, Diversified Mining Services*

"Richard is able to pass on his knowledge and experience in the recruitment industry in a meaningful and constructive way. He candidly shares some important insights which most others would refrain from doing." – *Graham Thomsen, Chair, Verterra Ecological Engineering*

"Richard is at the forefront in understanding the ever-changing recruitment industry in Australia, and once again he is ahead of the pack with his insightful thoughts and ideas on the new ways for Executives to find that role they really want. A must read for any Executive looking at a career change or taking the next step in their career." – *Bruce Myers, Former CEO, Lenards*

"Pragmatic, actionable, expert advice for the 21st Century. Richard Triggs gets C-suite recruitment in the modern 'digital' world. His advice is perfect for uncovering the hidden job market. Follow it, and the options available to you will appear." – *Nicholas Mathiou, Chief Executive Officer, Griffith Enterprise (Griffith University)*

"I was in a career rut, wondering what I wanted to do next. Then I attended Richard Triggs' 'Always Stand Out' seminar, implemented his tips, and within a month I was offered a great position." – *Sue Korecki, Principal, Environmental Assessment and Planning at Kleinfelder*

"Richard is recognised nationally for his innate ability to create quality C-suite and Board opportunities for Executives when to the naked eye little appears to be on the horizon." – *Frank Terranova, Chair, Taruga Gold Limited*

"Attending the workshop gave me startling insights to the relationship between employers, agents and job seekers. I was spell bound! As a result I radically rethought my strategy for finding my next role, came away feeling empowered and that I had gained a competitive advantage." – *Chris Langley, Project Manager, Arrow Energy*

"Richard Triggs has an exhaustive list of credentials in senior executive recruitment know-how, coaching and mentoring. His recent 'Always Stand Out' career workshop was inspirational and suitably attuned to today's needs for personal branding and social networking. I was also motivated through this workshop to engage Richard and his team as my personal ambassadors in finding my next career move." – *Fulvio Toniotti, Managing Director ANZ, GN Netcom*

"Richard's 'Always Stand Out' workshop enlightened me to the future of job search and career advancement. It taught me that I have the ability to significantly influence my career successes and I will benefit from taking direct action and control of my own destiny. If I don't, I'll get what I deserve!" – *David Blower, Non Executive Director, Queensland Chamber of Commerce and Industry*

"Richard's seminar was the most informative, humorous and insightful session on career search using social media in my career. The tools helped me transition from a technical role into consulting. Highly recommended and very reasonably priced." – *Kai Eberspaecher, Senior Associate, Advisian*

"Richard provides clear, sound and thought-provoking advice in relation to career guidance. His superior knowledge of the recruitment industry and extensive network allows him to speak with authority. Richard is regarded as market leader in the industry as he is highly regarded by his peers, competitors and employers as well as potential applicants." – *Keiran Travers, Senior Advisor, ETS Group*

"Those of us in the job market in 2015 will appreciate there has been a fundamental, and monumental, shift in approach by employers to sourcing candidates. Richard has identified this trend early and responded with an on-the-ball book full of practical and actionable tips which best positions readers for the current recruitment experience at all levels of an organisation. A must read!" – *Karen Taylor, Former Executive Manager, Suncorp*

"Richard's passion for helping people understand the power of the hidden job market knows no bounds, even when it comes to chastising his own industry! Anyone who is prepared to challenge the 'sacred cows' should be listened to. Richard is one of those people who needs to be listened to!" – *Neil James, Commercial Manager, HSE Mining*

"Richard is one of the leading authorities on the new, social media-based executive recruitment world which is fast devouring and replacing the old world of executive search and placement companies. You run the risk of going the way of the horse and cart if you ignore his message." – *Ross Willis, Chief Operating Officer, GVK Hancock*

"There has been a landscape shift in the way that management fills senior executive positions in the last few years and Richard is at the forefront of developing innovative methods for candidates to effectively get in the face of management for these positions, through the Always Stand Out workshops. The information presented at the workshops is practical and understandable and I would recommend them to anyone." – *Stuart Craig, Former Executive Director, Bid Operations, Gold Coast Commonwealth Games*

"I have used Richard's services on a number of occasions and found him to be exceptionally proactive and effective." – *Michael Klug, Chair, Queensland Rail and Autism Queensland*

"Richard has a refreshing, positive and successful approach in assisting and placing executives in their next career role. I congratulate him on the publishing of his book." – *Steve Roberts, Former Chairman, Linkwater*

"LinkedIn is the new way of affordable head hunting and job searching, and Richard Triggs has all the tips and tricks to make finding that new person/position a lot less stressful. I would highly recommend this read." – *Peter Anderson, Senior Executive, Property Solutions*

"I first came into contact with Richard when I left my role as a CEO with my last employer. Using techniques that Richard showed me in LinkedIn and more generally in my Job Search, I was able to make myself stand out for the quality candidate that I believed I was. I fairly rapidly secured the senior role I was seeking with a great company and people who I love working with and for. Thanks Richard for your clarity and excellent presentation of these key skills!" – *Scott Osborne, General Manager, Fit4Duty*

"If you are looking for a new career in 2015 and want some fundamental tips to successfully navigating, influencing, engaging and – ultimately – getting a job in the new world on recruiting, this is a must do. Richard Triggs' session is inspirational, highly informative and actionable. I highly recommend it." – *Damian Coren, Chief Marketing Officer, Global GBM*

ACKNOWLEDGEMENTS

Firstly, I would like to thank all of the organisations and executives that I have had the opportunity to work with as an Executive Recruiter and Career Coach over the last ten-plus years. It's been a crazy (and at times challenging) ride working in this industry, however it is great to be able to say that I still love what I do and my ability to be of service to you.

Secondly, thanks to my team of recruitment specialists, researchers and career coaches at Arete Executive, and in particular Tim Wallis. Tim, you have been a loyal friend and colleague and I am grateful every day for your efforts.

Thanks to the Key Person of Influence team who inspired, mentored and kicked my butt to get this book written. Glen Carlson, Andrew Griffiths and David Dugan, your support has been tremendous.

Heartfelt gratitude to my editor, Paul Slezak, my publisher, Michael Hanrahan, and all around marketing genius Natasha Howie – your contribution to this project has resulted in a book that I am truly proud of.

Finally, and most importantly, thank you to my business partner and wife, Fiona Cochran. Jack of all trades, and master of most (including being a great mum), none of this would have been possible without your love and support.

First published in 2015 by Richard Triggs

© 2015 Richard Triggs
The moral rights of the author have been asserted.

All rights reserved. This book may not be reproduced in whole or in part, stored, posted on the internet or transmitted in any form or by any means, electronic, mechanical, photocopying, recording, or other, without written permission from the publisher.

National Library of Australia Cataloguing-in-Publication entry:

Creator: Triggs, Richard, author.

Title: Uncover the hidden job market: how to find and win your next senior executive role

ISBN: 9780994218797 (paperback)

Subjects: Executives – Australia.
           Executives – Training of – Australia.
           Executives – Recruiting – Australia.
           Career development – Australia.

Dewey Number: 658.407111

Cover and internal design by Penny Black Design
Book production by Michael Hanrahan Publishing
Printed in Australia by McPherson's Printing

The material in this publication is of the nature of general comment only, and does not represent professional advice. It is not intended to provide specific guidance for particular circumstances and it should not be relied on as the basis for any decision to take action or not take action on any matter which it covers. Readers should obtain professional advice where appropriate, before making any such decision. To the maximum extent permitted by law, the author and publisher disclaim all responsibility and liability to any person, arising directly or indirectly from any person taking or not taking action based on the information in this publication.

CONTENTS

Introduction **1**

1 The Future of Recruitment **9**

2 What Do You Want To Do When You Grow Up?
How To Work Out What Your Preferred
Next Career Move Looks Like **19**

3 Standing Out From The Crowd **29**

4 Connecting Directly With Your Employers Of Choice **45**

5 How To Achieve The Best Possible Outcomes
Working With Recruitment Consultants **69**

6 How To Stay Motivated During Your Job Search Process **85**

7 How To Perform At Your Best During A Job Interview **97**

8 How To Manage The Job Offer Process **111**

9 Showing Appreciation To Those Who
Helped Along The Way **129**

Conclusion **133**

INTRODUCTION

I'm guessing you have opened this book because you're looking for a new job. Maybe you have been made redundant (or terminated – don't worry, it's happened to me too!); maybe you are currently employed but looking for a career move – more responsibility, more flexibility, more money, or a change of location; maybe you've just obtained some new qualifications and you are looking for a complete change – a new job in a new industry.

Whatever your circumstances, firstly let me say thank you for taking the time to investigate this book and what it can offer you. I feel confident that if you commit yourself to reading it (after all, time is precious and you could be doing other things), then by the end you will have a much higher level of confidence that you can "headhunt your own job", and end up with a new role that you are really happy with.

As well as being a job seeker like you in my past, I founded and became the Managing Partner of one of Australia's leading executive recruitment companies, Arete Executive. From our inception, one of our key priorities was being at the forefront of new technologies and methodologies for identifying and headhunting the best talent for our clients. Having completed hundreds of recruitment assignments for senior leadership roles, I've literally met thousands of executive job seekers looking for their next opportunity.

This book represents the distillation of everything I have learned as an executive recruiter, translated into a clear and concise template that if you follow, will definitely help you to more quickly secure your next job. You'll be able to proactively target your employers of choice and access the elusive "hidden job market", often spoken about but rarely understood properly.

You'll also learn how to become an expert at using LinkedIn specifically to position yourself as a preferred candidate for career opportunities, using a number of tools to Search Engine Optimise your LinkedIn profile. You'll end up with an excellent LinkedIn profile that will make employers and executive recruiters keen to engage with you.

This book will also assist you in learning how to develop excellent relationships with executive recruiters who work in your chosen industry. You'll be amazed at how easy it is to become a preferred candidate and be leveraged into opportunities by those executive recruiters that you invest in developing a great relationship with, yet so few job seekers actually make the effort to do this.

This book is definitely going to ask you to do some things that push you outside of your comfort zone. You are going to have to "take the bull by the horns" and get yourself in front of your employers of choice, before they even know they need you. You are going to have to be proactive (without being pushy) in developing relationships with recruiters and also key people of influence within your chosen profession.

> You have to become an expert at articulating your key achievements and transferable skills. Very few candidates can do this well, so if you take the time to work this out at the beginning of your job search you will definitely have a distinct advantage when you start to get out in the market.

One of the points I am going to make many times in this book is that you have to become an expert at articulating your key achievements and transferable skills. Very few candidates can do this well, so if you take the time to work this out at the beginning of your job search you will definitely have a distinct advantage when you start to get out in the market, updating your LinkedIn profile and CV, and speaking with recruiters and employers.

So what do I mean by this? You may have heard the expression, "you sell the sizzle not the steak". This is one of those old sales training clichés, but for those unfamiliar with the expression, here's my version.

Imagine you walk into your local suburban restaurant, and on the menu is "Steak and Chips – $25.00". No information about the cut of steak, or the way it is cooked. Just an item and a price.

Alternatively, imagine this scenario. You walk into one of the best steak restaurants in town. Once seated at a table with an immaculate tablecloth and beautiful cutlery and glassware, the waiter tells you the special of the day:

"Today we have a unique cut of eye fillet steak, that the chef has had personally flown in especially for this restaurant. This steak is extremely rare to source because of the unique conditions that the cattle are grazed in. This steak comes from a herd that grazes on the east-facing side of Mount Everest, and eats a pure diet of fresh grass that is hand planted by a team of Nepalese Buddhist monks. Each cow has its own name and personal servant for its entire life, and lives in blissful harmony, blessed each day by the head monk. The meat is then aged in a snow cave higher up in Mount Everest, for 120 days. Each day it is rubbed in a secret herbal recipe passed down for over 700 years. The steaks are then packed in ice and flown directly here, before being slow cooked over the coals of a unique mix of timbers and mosses, giving it a truly unique flavour and melt in your mouth texture, all for the very special price of $95.00". And if you want the hand cut chips cooked in duck fat, that will be an extra $15.00.

Now the reality is that the $95 steak is probably not much better that the $25 steak, certainly not for almost four times the price. Yet business people and the wealthy line up every day to buy the $95 steak. If you don't believe me, watch all the cooking shows like Gordon Ramsay, Heston Blumenthal and the like. People love the experience, the unique and exotic tastes, and most importantly they want to feel special. So they pay $95 for a steak when a $25 one would have been just as nutritionally equivalent and probably would have tasted almost (if not) as nice.

So you need to become an expert at being able to clearly articulate your key achievements and transferable skills, so that you can sell your "sizzle" and not just your "steak". Quantifiable (i.e. measurable) achievements are the key here, which really demonstrate why you are excellent at your job.

"Increased turnover by 317% in the 2013/2014 financial year"

"Reduced staff turnover by 47% over five years"

"Launched a new product which captured 26% of market share within the first 12 months"

"Awarded employee of the year for three consecutive years" etc.

Sometimes you will be applying for jobs where you have not done exactly the same things in your prior career. This is why I refer to your transferable skills. What I mean here is that you give thought to what the new role requires, and what is your most relevant previous experience. Then you proactively share your prior experience as a way of being able to demonstrate you can do the new tasks.

Looking for a new job can be daunting. You are going to have to put yourself out into the market, and will probably face the discomfort of being "rejected" for jobs that you are really keen on. You'll get frustrated dealing with recruiters that don't understand your value proposition and regularly don't fulfil your expectations regarding being treated well (phone calls not returned, emails not replied to and general poor service). You'll be interviewed by hiring managers that seem disinterested, disengaged and unresponsive. Unless you are really fortunate, you'll take at least a few knocks to your self-confidence.

So another point I am going to make many times is that you are AWESOME! Don't forget that you have achieved great things for your employers and your peers and teams in your career. Don't forget that there are many companies out there that would feel blessed to have you working in their business. You are a proven performer, you are a great team player, and you get results. You are AWESOME!

Let me tell you that I have presented this information both one-on-one and in seminars to hundreds of senior executives. Those people that take the advice and take action have achieved fantastic results. Those that simply sit back and wait for the job to be advertised on Seek or other job boards will be waiting a very long time to secure their next role, and often need to make lots of compromises along the way compared to what is truly their job of choice with their employer of choice.

Which one are you? The person who wants to take immediate and massive action to create their preferred job, or the person who wants to sit back and pray it comes to them? I hope you are the former, as this book will guide you in how to accelerate your job search exponentially compared to virtually every other candidate out there looking for a new job.

There is a saying I really like:

There are those who make it happen
There are those who watch it happen
There are those who wonder, "What happened?"

If you want to make it happen, at least in relation to being able to "uncover the hidden job market", then keep reading and most importantly implementing the tools and techniques you'll learn in this book. You'll end up with an excellent job, and the investment of time in reading this book will have been extremely worthwhile.

You'll note that this book has been specifically targeted towards executives seeking roles on salaries of $200,000 per annum or more. This is not because I am trying to be elitist, it's just that this market is where I have had the most experience as both an executive recruiter and career coach. I have placed well over 500 senior executives at this salary level and much higher (up to $1m salary packages), and coached one-on-one and in seminars literally thousands of these executives, during my career as an executive recruitment specialist.

The success stories that are shared in this book are mainly about senior executives at this salary level. (Please note: names have been changed to protect confidentiality.) However the tools that you will learn in this book are equally applicable to any job search, no matter the role type or salary level.

1
THE FUTURE OF RECRUITMENT

The recruitment industry has gone through significant change over the last few years. At a macro-economic level, the world has been dealing with an unstable employment market, driven by the Global Financial Crisis and subsequent challenging economic environment, and other more local and national issues.

So the last five years have been tough, with 2013/14 particularly so. When economic uncertainty is high, and business confidence is low, then the perceived risk of a career change is also high for many executives. So lots of people, who would have changed jobs/employers in a more positive market, chose instead to remain in their current roles. Even though in their own minds they were ready and wanted a change, they deemed the risk too high, so they stayed put.

This means that the recruitment activity that would happen in a better market, to fill the roles vacated by people moving on to bigger and better opportunities, has been almost non-existant. Coupled with certain industries going through contraction and resultant redundancies, the employment market looks gloomy indeed.

The economic outlook is now far more positive (regardless of what the newspapers say), the employment market has significantly improved, employers are starting to grow their teams, and most importantly the people who were hesitant to change employment are now more confident and therefore more active in their job search. All this is good news for job seekers.

However, there is another factor that has completely changed the recruitment landscape, and that is LinkedIn. Five years ago LinkedIn was starting to get some traction with executive headhunters (including yours truly) as a talent-sourcing tool. In fact, in 2009/2010, I personally built a LinkedIn network of over 17,000 direct LinkedIn connections, purely so that I could "see" almost 30 million profiles of LinkedIn users (at that time you could only see profiles within three degrees of separation – more on this later). This became my candidate database and Arete Executive filled almost all of our recruitment assignments with candidates sourced directly from LinkedIn.

Your LinkedIn Network

17,233 Connections

27,348,745 Professionals in your Network

Add connections

Fast forward to the last 12 months or so, and LinkedIn now offers a special subscription license called LinkedIn Recruiter, which allows the subscriber complete visibility of all profiles globally on the LinkedIn network (thus making my 17,000 direct connections largely irrelevant). Larger employers have quickly taken up these LinkedIn Recruiter licenses, and in-house recruitment teams have become far more competent at using LinkedIn as a sourcing tool for filling their own vacancies.

Using recruitment consultants is not dissimilar to paying for parking. When you are driving into the city for an important meeting, often you need to pay a hefty fee to use a centrally located parking facility. Nobody excitedly says, "Wow, I just paid $60 to park my car for two hours, what an awesome investment!" Parking is a regrettable spend. You're in a hurry, you appreciate the convenience of being able to park close to your appointment, but you certainly aren't excited about paying the fee.

Likewise is paying for a third-party recruitment consultant to present candidates for your vacancy.

Let's assume a mining company wants to hire a new CFO, and the salary is $300,000 per annum. A tier-one global search company could charge between 30 and 40 percent of the salary for managing this assignment. For the sake of this illustration, let's say they use a local provider who offers to do the work for 20 percent of the package, or $60,000 (20 percent of $300k).

Now $60k in anyone's language is a lot of money. No employer is excited about paying this fee (it's a regrettable spend), however in the past they were obliged to, because the recruitment consultant who specialises in identifying and placing CFOs has the database of candidates, and the employer wants these candidates. Your typical employer does not perceive that the recruitment consultant adds much, if any, value to the process. In fact, many employers regard recruitment consultants in the same light as used car salespeople, or simply "body shoppers".

However, the situation is now very different. Probably 95 percent of white-collar professionals have a LinkedIn profile, including CFOs. So the mining company says to their $60k per annum internal recruitment resource (often an early career HR graduate or an external recruiter who has gone in-house to avoid the pressures of sales targets etc.), *"Mary, we want you to find the details of every CFO at every ASX listed mining company based in Brisbane. Preferably CPA qualified, preferably 15 plus years experience, preferably having worked in one of the major underground coal mining companies".*

Mary jumps onto LinkedIn using her Recruiter license, and using a few keyword searches she can easily and very quickly complete the list. She then shows the profiles to her boss, they agree on which individuals to target, and the recruitment process begins. So instead of the mining company paying $60k for one placement, they can employ Mary for an entire year, and get much greater bang for their buck.

> The poor old traditional recruiter is, in my opinion, dying a certain and unavoidable death, never to be resuscitated. Their entire value proposition has been eroded, because for the first time ever, employers have direct access to their prospective candidate pool, easily and cheaply.

So the poor old traditional recruiter is, in my opinion, dying a certain and unavoidable death, never to be resuscitated. Their entire value proposition has been eroded, because for the first time ever, through using LinkedIn employers have direct access to their prospective candidate pool, easily and cheaply. Just like MYOB had a profound impact on the accounting profession, LinkedIn is now the same catalyst for change within the recruitment industry.

Recently I met with and interviewed the Chief Human Resources Officer (or equivalent) of many of the ASX top 50 companies, as part of my research for this book. Without exception, every single one of them said that their current strategy was to in-source their entire recruitment capability, and only use external recruiters as a matter of absolute last recourse. Most said that they were consistently able to fill greater than 90 percent of their vacancies without any reliance on external recruitment companies. When I offered my opinion that the traditional external recruitment provider was dead, never to be resuscitated, they agreed immediately and completely.

Not great news for my peers within the recruitment industry. If you are a job seeker and you go and meet with a recruitment consultant, I can almost guarantee that they will tell you the employment market is bad, there's little if any activity, and your prospects for finding a new job are limited.

Quite honestly, this is absolute rubbish.

The market is strong and good candidates are easily finding good work. However, these opportunities are rarely coming through traditional recruitment consultants. Either the candidate is being approached directly by the employer, or the candidate is proactively getting in front of the employer, and accessing the hidden job market.

Just as LinkedIn now means that employers no longer require recruitment consultants to access their candidates, likewise candidates no longer require recruitment consultants to access their employers of choice.

Up until recently, recruitment consultants made a lot of money by "showcasing talent", or "floating" candidates, to their employers of choice. For example, I recruited predominantly in the property development industry. Let's say that a Senior Development Manager from Stockland came to see me saying they wanted a new job. Maybe they had outgrown their existing role, no longer had a positive relationship with their boss, or perhaps they wanted to move geographically. I would say to them that I could present them to a range of other employers, including Lend Lease, Australand, Devine and the like.

I'd then contact the relevant employer and offer to arrange for them to meet my candidate, on the basis that if the meeting went well and they subsequently employed that person, then I would be paid a substantial fee. And pay they would, because in a booming market, with no direct access to candidates, the employer would have no other option.

Nowadays, it is very rare for an employer to have the meeting under the obligation of needing to pay a substantial fee should they choose to employ the candidate. However if they could have the meeting and then employ for free (i.e. with no recruitment fees applied) then they will do so every day of the week.

I recently tested this assumption at a workshop I ran for 83 senior executive leaders. I asked the group whether, if contacted directly by a legitimate, well-qualified executive to discuss the executive's interest in joining their business, they would have the meeting? Every single one of them said yes. I then asked them how often they were approached on this basis, and they said rarely if ever.

This is the greatest opportunity for you as a job seeker. Identify your target employers of choice, approach the relevant executive line manager you are most likely to report to directly, and get in front of them before they know they need you. This is how to access the hidden job market. LinkedIn gives you immediate and direct access like never before. This is the premise of this book, and how you can headhunt your own perfect job. This book is going to show you exactly how to do this for best results.

In this chapter, I've shown you that:

- Economic conditions globally have significantly impacted the recruitment market over the last few years
- New technologies, in particular LinkedIn, are having a profound and irrevocable effect on how organisations are recruiting senior executives
- The full impact of LinkedIn is now starting to be felt by the recruitment industry, with traditional executive recruitment companies struggling to remain relevant and facing a very challenging future
- The onus is now on senior executives to become very proactive in how they utilise tools such as LinkedIn to access the hidden job market and secure future opportunities.

CASE STUDY #1:

How Terry, a Senior Process Engineer, Grew His LinkedIn Network from 70 to 400 in 30 Days

Summary:

I found myself out of work in 2013 and the job market had changed so much I was worried that I would never find a new job. I worked with recruitment agents, who provided no help. Then, I started trying to use LinkedIn, but I was unfamiliar with how it worked and how it could help me find a job. After doing some searches for "career coaching," I came across the details of Richard Triggs' seminar, "Always Stand Out." I attended his seminar and learned so much about taking advantage of social media and the networking opportunities available. His information led me to change my approach, specifically on LinkedIn. After the seminar, I used Richard's recommendations and I was able to grow my LinkedIn network from 70 to more than 400 in just 30 days.

The Problem:

Through my 30 years as a process engineer, I had only been out of work a couple of times. In the past, I never had a problem finding work, but in 2013, I was out of work and suddenly realizing the job market had changed significantly. Over three months I applied for more than 30 jobs and I did not even get to the interview stage. When I connected with former colleagues, I found that many were dealing with the same problem I was.

To boost my job searching efforts, I started working with recruitment agents. While I received calls from agents weekly, I did not hear back from them. I contacted recruitment agents after they submitted my resume to companies, only to hear that the market was competitive and the company found someone with better qualifications. It did not seem like the agents were really serious about helping me find a job. In fact, one recruiter emailed me and asked for my CV for an urgent job opening. Unfortunately, after he had my CV, I never heard from the recruiter again.

I had joined LinkedIn in the past and I started working to update my details, but I was not aware of how to use the professional networking site. By March 2014, I realised that my efforts on LinkedIn were not getting me anywhere, since I was not sure how to contact potential employers or how to network with others on LinkedIn.

The Solution:

As I started searching using various keywords, one day I used the search term, "career coaching." That is when I stumbled across Richard Triggs and his seminar, "Always Stand Out." At first, I did not think that the seminar was for me, even though it sounded interesting. I did not know much about using social media and did not know if it would really help me. However, as I thought about the seminar, I realised that something had to change. I was out of options.

I decided to give Richard's seminar a try. At the seminar, I met others dealing with similar problems in the job market, even though they had plenty of job experience. Richard's seminar explained how the job market had changed, as well as the importance of social media. He also explained how job seekers could begin taking advantage of the social media tools offered by LinkedIn. New networking strategies were laid out, showing me how I could become competitive, even in a tough job market. Most of all, I started feeling hope that I could find a job, which gave me the direction I needed to start making changes.

After attending the "Always Stand Out" seminar, I started to implement many of the recommendations offered by Richard. I did not find it easy – I really had to step out of my comfort zone, since I am not really a person who likes to promote myself. However, I knew I had to make changes, so I began using the LinkedIn suggestions for optimizing my profile and building connections with other professionals. Richard's seminar taught me how to search LinkedIn for potential influential contacts, and then, how to approach those individuals with a job pitch.

The Results:

By following Richard's suggestions, I was able to grow my network quickly. Within just 30 days, my network went from 70 to more than 400 people. Not only did my network grow, but I also saw a huge increase in profile views.

Using Richard's approach changed how I used LinkedIn, with great results, and it also made me feel more empowered as I searched for a new job. Richard's seminar did make me feel more confident, which helped me land a great job. Whilst the job I got came from applying to an advert and not from LinkedIn directly, it is entirely possible that my new employer checked out my new, improved LinkedIn profile.

In the end, it was Richard's advice that reinvigorated me in my search for a job. It provided me with the hope I needed to continue trying, which is an essential part of successfully finding a job in the current job market. I learned that I needed to act and think differently, since the job market has changed significantly within the past decade. I have learned new ways to connect with professionals and exciting job search techniques that make me stand out from other talent in the job market.

2
WHAT DO YOU WANT TO DO WHEN YOU GROW UP?
How To Work Out What Your Preferred Next Career Move Looks Like

One of the first exercises I take senior executives through when meeting with them to discuss their desire to find a new job is to try and narrow down what that new job actually looks like; i.e. what is their job of choice with their employer of choice?

A great way to get the conversation started is with the following illustration:

Quadrant One:	Quadrant Two:
• Same Job	• Different Job
• Same Industry	• Same Industry
Quadrant Three:	**Quadrant Four:**
• Same Job	• Different Job
• Different Industry	• Different Industry

Let's use two hypothetical job seekers as a way of illustrating how this works:

Sally is currently a Sales Manager in a Property Services Company. Steven is currently a Finance Manager in a Mining Company.

Quadrant One – Same Job/Same Industry

In this quadrant, the job seeker loves their current responsibilities and their current industry. Instead of seeking a significant change in their career, they simply want to move into a different organisation, or be promoted within their current one. Maybe they want more money, more responsibility, more work/life flexibility, or perhaps they are moving to a new city/country. Maybe they are just sick of their boss, a colleague or another aspect of where they currently work.

Sally still wants to be a Sales Manager in a Property Services Company. Steven still wants to be a Finance Manager in a Mining Company.

Quadrant Two – Different Job/Same Industry

This is the quadrant where someone wants a change of pace, with new tasks and goals to achieve, whilst remaining in the same industry in which they currently work. This is the only quadrant that allows for someone to remain with his or her current employer, whilst moving into a different role family.

Sally enjoys the Property Services industry, however after many years in Sales she wants to move into an Operations Management role, or maybe a Marketing role.

Steven likewise enjoys the Mining industry, however he wants to move into Risk Management, or Mergers and Acquisitions, for example.

Quadrant Three – Same Job/Different Industry

This is the quadrant where someone loves what he or she currently does, however they are bored with the industry they work in and want a new challenge. This type of career transition is quite common, because a lot of skill sets are easily transferable across industries, especially if the candidate can prove some great career successes that demonstrate their ability to adapt and perform in different environments.

Sally wants to take her sales and leadership skills into the Event Management industry, or perhaps the Financial Services industry.

Steven wants to take his finance skills into the Construction industry, or perhaps the Not For Profit sector.

Quadrant Four – Different Job/Different Industry

This final quadrant is where someone wants a complete change. Often a catalyst for this type of change is completing some new qualifications, especially an MBA. In fact this was my own experience. After many years in the Property Services industry (starting in sales and then moving into operational management roles), I completed an Executive MBA. My boss at the time (the company's CEO) had just turned 50, had taken equity in the company I was working for, and was not going anywhere anytime soon (in fact he's still there and doing a great job). Realising my promotion opportunities would be non-existent, I went to see a recruiter I had been a client of, and asked him to help me find a new job. He suggested joining him in the recruitment industry and as they say, the rest is history!

I would say that a high proportion of senior executives who now come and see me, initially see this quadrant as holding a lot of appeal. They have spent years building their career within one particular industry and are completely bored, burnt out, or just wanting something new and fun to do. However there are some important things to note when assessing whether a new job in a new industry is really for you.

Firstly, as an individual you have built a personal brand in your industry that brings with it a degree of authority, credibility and experience. This reflects directly in the level of seniority you hold, the level of your accountability, and ultimately the amount of income you earn. Changing roles and industries simultaneously can have a significant impact on this.

For example, I used to have commercial lawyers regularly coming to see me because I specialised in recruiting into the Property Development industry, and they fancied themselves as the future leaders of Development companies, maybe because they had renovated a house, done a "block split" (where you separate a residential block into two separate titles, allowing you to sell one or both and make a profit), or perhaps they handled the legal work on some property transactions. These lawyers saw the development industry as sexy, where massive deals and profits could be made, and they wanted in.

When faced with the very real prospect that because they had no formal property qualifications or real development experience, they realised they would need to essentially start their career again. Often this would be in a very junior role and on a much lower salary than they were used to. At this point, they almost always made the (smart) decision to remain in their same job/same industry.

The second important thing to note when considering new job/ new industry is that at least on paper (i.e. an applicant's CV), there will always be a better-qualified candidate than you. So if you are applying for roles where you have no relevant professional background, unless you are extremely capable of communicating your key achievements and transferable skills, it is highly unlikely that you will even get consideration by a recruiter, let alone being interviewed and then offered the job.

95 percent of recruitment consultants are nothing more than order takers. They meet with their client, who dictates the requirements for the role.

The main reason for this is that 95 percent of recruitment consultants are nothing more than order takers. They meet with their client, who dictates the requirements for the role. Because the recruiter is not skilled at truly exploring and questioning the brief, and because they are not perceived by their client as a trusted advisor, they end up with a shopping list of background requirements that may look something like this:

Client – "I need a new sales manager for my building products company. They must have a minimum of 15 years' experience, have formal business qualifications, have lead teams of at least 20 salespeople, and have worked previously in one of these specific competitor organisations..."

Unless the recruiter pushes back on some of these prerequisites and perhaps challenges some of the client's perspectives (which is rarely if ever the case), then that becomes the criteria for reviewing all potential applicants. Quite simply, they are looking to put a square peg in a square hole.

Statistics say that CVs submitted in response to a job advertisement on average are viewed for 15 seconds by the recruitment consultant. Essentially they are looking for reasons to discount you from further consideration, rather than find reasons to include you, simply as a way of dealing with the massive volumes of CVs received (for a sales role this could easily be over 200 applications). So unless in the 15 seconds your CV gets looked at, it clearly demonstrates that you match their client's criteria, you are most likely going to receive the dreaded "thanks but no thanks" letter (actually these letters are your friends, as you'll discover later in this book).

I am certainly not suggesting that you should not consider a new job/new industry move. In fact, as long as you are happy with perhaps taking less salary or holding less responsibility when learning your new craft, then I absolutely encourage it. You simply need to adopt an entirely different approach to your job search process. You need to get in front of your employer of choice before they know that they even need you. This way you are not being compared to 200 other applicants; you are simply being considered on your own merits. Do you pass the "good bloke/woman" test, and how compelling are your key achievements and transferable skills?

Once again, what we are talking about here is accessing the hidden job market, the central theme of this book, and what you will soon become an expert in doing.

In this chapter, you've learned that:

- There are four distinct paths you can consider when deciding on your next role: same job/same industry; different job/same industry; same job/different industry; and different job/different industry

- Each pathway has its own unique opportunities and challenges to be considered

- The further you choose to stray from same job/same industry, the greater onus will be on you to create your own opportunities, as recruiters just want to "fill square holes with square pegs".

CASE STUDY #2:

How Peter, a Senior Marketing Manager, Landed His New Job with XYZ Industries (company name confidential)

Summary:

After taking a break from work, it was time to head back, since I was dealing with boredom. I started my job search by calling multiple Executive Search firms, spoke with multiple recruitment agencies and created a LinkedIn Profile. Since I did not receive help from the Executive Search firms or the recruitment agencies, I had to try a new approach. When attending the "Always Stand Out" seminar with Richard Triggs one piece of advice really stood out – find a company you really want to work for, call the MD and sell yourself. I followed that advice and pursued a job with XYZ Industries. It started out with an initial three-month consulting gig and ended with a full-time job with the company.

The Problem:

When I decided it was time to head back to work, I used several methods to start searching for a new job. I began talking with the best Executive Search firms I could find, but since the firms could not really put me in a box, they were not able to help me. Every time they asked me what my ideal job was, I told them I wanted to work with a startup company so I could get involved in actually building something instead of working with a company that had an existing marketing team and customer base. However, that information did not seem to make sense to the Executive Search firms and I did not enjoy any results – they didn't find me one job opportunity.

I also talked with some recruitment agencies, but once again, I did not see results. While the recruitment agencies gave me many promises, they provided no help. Most of the recruitment firms never returned my phone calls and they did not provide me with any feedback either.

In my job search, I did join LinkedIn and started looking at job seeker websites. However, I did not have any luck with the job seeker sites and my limited efforts on LinkedIn did not provide any results either. I was stumped and not sure where to turn as I looked for a new job.

The Solution:

After seeing no results, despite all my efforts, I heard about the "Always Stand Out" seminar offered by Richard Triggs. I attended the seminar and enjoyed all the information provided. However, out of all the excellent advice and tips, one thing really stood out to me. His advice was to find a company that you really want to work for, call the MD and then tell the MD why he should hire you for the success of his company.

After the seminar, this piece of advice was stuck in my head. Earlier in the year I had read an article about XYZ Industries, a junior mining company that was raising money to re-commission a graphite mine located in South Australia. I had kept the article and I decided that I would really like to work for this company. I took Richard's advice and called the XYZ Industries MD. I shared my background, experience and the benefits I could bring to the company. He requested my resume and a few weeks later, he offered to employ me as a temporary consultant. If the company were happy with my work, then they would offer me a fulltime job.

After that conversation, I did not hear from the MD, since he was away on business. During that time, I had the opportunity to speak at an International Conference. It was located in Hungary and I was to speak about Magnesia. I accepted the speaking gig and thought it was a great time to contact XYZ Industries again. I let them know about the speaking engagement and told them that their target customers would be at the conference. If they added me as a consultant, they could save thousands in expenses and I would be able to talk to those target customers while at the conference.

The Results:

Once I talked with the company and informed them how I could help them by dealing with target customers at my speaking engagement in Hungary, in a week I had an agreement to work with the company as a temporary consultant for three months.

I completed the three months as a temporary consultant and XYZ Industries hired me fulltime. Now I can still work from my beach office, I get to enjoy travelling and I'm working for a startup company where I really feel that I'm making a big difference. I love working for a small company. Each day I face different challenges, which keeps me from being bored.

When all my other job seeking efforts failed to provide results, it was the "Always Stand Out" seminar that pushed me to go after a job I really wanted. I do not think I would have pursued this job so actively had I not attended the seminar by Richard Triggs. Just a single piece of advice was enough to push me out of my comfort zone, helping me land my dream job.

3
STANDING OUT
FROM THE CROWD

As mentioned previously, LinkedIn is now the predominant candidate-sourcing tool utilised by both internal and external recruiters. This is why newspaper job advertisements are now almost non-existent, and even advertising on job boards like Seek has sharply declined (at least for some sectors). Why advertise a role and potentially get 200 plus applicants, 190 of which are not suitable and won't get interviewed, when you can search LinkedIn, find your preferred ten candidates and contact them directly?

> Your LinkedIn profile is your CV in the current job market. It will get viewed much more often than your CV could, because it is available in the public domain.

Your LinkedIn profile is your CV in the current job market. It will get viewed much more often than your CV could, because it is available in the public domain. It can easily be found by recruiters, using keyword searches for those attributes requested by the employer. In addition, you can have a LinkedIn profile visible without directly advertising that you are looking for a new job, versus posting a CV, which makes it obvious that you are an active job seeker (something that you probably don't want from a confidentiality perspective, especially if you are currently employed).

So as a job seeker, the first thing you need to do is have an excellent LinkedIn profile; one that is easily found by recruiters, that is "sexy" and best represents you as an attractive candidate, and ultimately encourages recruiters to contact you about job opportunities.

There is a new concept in online marketing called the Zero Moment of Truth (ZMOT). Jim Lecinski from Google has written an excellent eBook, *Winning the Zero Moment of Truth* (2011) which I would definitely recommend reading to learn more about this concept.

The Zero Moment of Truth is the first time a potential buyer (employer) seeks information about a particular product (employee). The internet is allowing buyers to be able to seek information and opinions about things they want to buy, before they make any attempt to actually engage in a sales process.

To use a consumer marketing example, let's say you want to buy some new toothpaste. When you go into the supermarket, and see the toothpaste on the shelf, that is the First Moment of Truth, when you decide if you will buy it. Once you buy the toothpaste and take it home, the Second Moment of Truth is when you use the toothpaste and decide how satisfied you are with the experience and product.

As Jim Lecinski writes, *"Today's consumers know so much more before they reach the shelf. They find incredible detail online, from every possible source, about the brands and products that matter to them. They browse, dig, explore, dream and master, and then they're ready to buy with confidence. And what they* learn, they share with others…those Zero Moments of Truth where first impressions happen and the path to purchase often begins."

How does ZMOT apply to your job search? Well, the Zero Moment of Truth is when someone looks at your LinkedIn profile (plus potentially other readily available information about you on the internet). They are forming an opinion about you before they even see your CV or have a conversation about you or with you.

When a prospective employer (or recruitment consultant) looks at your LinkedIn profile, they are asking themselves, "*Can this person make me and/or save me money? Can they make my life easier? Can they solve the problems I am currently experiencing in my business?*" So you need to make sure that your LinkedIn profile can pre-emptively answer these questions as quickly and positively as possible, as they apply to your job of choice with your employer of choice.

Now, there are many books written about how to write an excellent LinkedIn profile, just as there are about how to write an excellent CV. (One great book is *I'm On LinkedIn, Now What?* by Jason Alba.) As such, I'm not going to focus much on that here, apart from making a few key statements.

> Your LinkedIn profile should be as good as, if not better than your current CV. It should contain as much content as possible, to best articulate your key achievements and transferable skills.

Firstly, your LinkedIn profile should be as good as, if not better than your current CV. It should contain as much content as possible, to best articulate your key achievements and transferable skills. It should have a good quality headshot photograph of you in a professional setting (i.e. not running a marathon, playing with your dog, etc.). You should include plenty of detail on each of your historical roles, your professional qualifications, and any professional memberships.

Now for the lesser known stuff about how to have a great LinkedIn profile. Essentially, how to Search Engine Optimise (SEO) your profile so that when recruiters are running keyword searches (which they can and will be doing), you have the best chance of being one of the first profiles they see.

Google makes a lot of money from the concept of SEO. Imagine you are looking for a certain service in a certain area. For example, you want a dentist close to where you live. You go to Google and type in "Dentist South Brisbane" and up comes a list of providers in that area. Most likely, you'll look at the first few that come up before making a selection, and very rarely if ever go past the first page of the Google searched websites.

Companies can pay very large amounts of money to ensure that their website is Search Engine Optimised and is virtually guaranteed to come up in the top five when someone does a Google search on their respective service offering. There are consultants who specialise in SEO, and Google has a range of analytical tools to assist in SEO, plus "pay per click" advertising, and other tools.

Likewise, if you are a Civil Engineer who specialises in road construction in Brisbane, you want to SEO your LinkedIn profile to make sure you come up at the top (or certainly on the first page) when a recruiter is searching for this skill set on LinkedIn. The good news is that this is easy to do, and won't cost you a cent (other than the cost of this book, of course).

What you want to do is consider what are the keywords that best represent your skill set and the job that you want. You then want to make sure that these words appear in your profile **a lot** (although not so much that it looks and reads badly, which would actually detract from your appeal to recruiters).

The Civil Engineer who specialises in road construction in Brisbane, will ensure that his job title specifically says that. His profile summary will use those phrases multiple times. Each of his roles will feature those words multiple times, both in the job title and the job descriptions.

Here's an example of an SEO optimised profile, being mine.

Richard Triggs
Managing Partner of Arete Executive, Executive Search Specialist and Career Coach
richardt@areteexecutive.com.au

Summary
Managing Partner of Arete Executive, Executive Search Specialist and Career Coach

Richard commenced his executive search career after eleven years working within the property industry in senior executive business development and operational management roles. Having now been an executive search consultant for over twelve years, he has also held senior leadership roles within the executive search industry.

Richard has conducted executive search assignments for senior executives and board members throughout Australia and internationally. His executive search clients range from SMEs to multi-national listed organisations.

Examples of executive search assignments that Richard and his team have completed include: Chairperson, Non Executive Director, CEO, COO, CFO, CIO, Executive Director, Executive General Manager, through to mid-level executive leaders across all functions within an organisation.

Richard has completed a Bachelor of Commerce degree majoring in Marketing and Human Resources Management and a Masters in Business Administration. He was the inaugural President of the Brisbane Executive Club, QUT's MBA alumni association.

Richard is also a qualified executive career coach and has provided career coaching to many senior leaders in both their job search process and ongoing work performance. Richard regularly presents to Griffith University, Queensland University of Technology, Australian Institute of Management and other industry groups around executive search and career coaching related issues.

Richard is a Fellow of AIM, a member of AICD and an alumni member of Queensland Leaders.

Specialties: Executives search assignments for senior level, strategic executive search primarily in the Australian market, plus the delivery of executive career coaching programmes that have been designed to assist senior leaders and managers with their own career direction and those of their team.

Experience

Managing Partner, Executive Search Specialist and Career Coach at Arete Executive - Executive Search and Career Coaching
February 2009 - Present (5 years 10 months)

Arete Executive is a true Executive Search specialist. A boutique "headhunter", Arete identifies who's who in the marketplace via our unique search process, engages with high-calibre candidates and connects them to their employer of choice. Working with an executive search Performance-Based Hiring methodology and search process, we attract highly-renowned leaders to business critical senior management and executive roles for our clients. Our world best practice executive search capability allows us to pursue both active and passive candidates across Australia and the world to produce an extensive, targeted candidate list for each executive search assignment. Simply, we listen to our clients and search the entire market to bring them the most skilled executive personnel for the job.

With unrivalled executive search experience, the Arete team has its finger on the pulse of Australian business having built strong networks with executive leaders across a wide range of industries including: Mining, Energy Oil & Gas, Property & Construction, Professional Services and C-suite and Board roles e.g.: CEO, CFO, MD. For our executive search clients, Arete is a trusted strategic advisor, providing them with invaluable market intelligence.

4 recommendations available upon request

Associate Partner - Executive Search at Luminary Search (Executive Search division of Chandler Macleod Group)

July 2008 - February 2009 (8 months)

Luminary Executive Search is the International Executive Search business of the Chandler Macleod Group (CMG), one of the World's largest recruitment and Human Resource Outsource organisations. Richard joined the organisation to head their global property and construction executive search practice.

This was a senior executive role within the group. Richard successfully undertook and placed numerous executive level positions across his target industries utilising his extensive executive search skills and industry executive contacts.

18 recommendations available upon request

Executive Director - Executive Search Specialist at Davidson Recruitment

November 2003 - May 2008 (4 years 7 months)

Richard was a senior executive leader within this highily-regarded recruitment and search business.

He carried out successful executive search assignments across sectors including: Property & Construction, Engineering, Mining, Supply Chain Procurement, IT&T, Banking and Finance.

17 recommendations available upon request

Recruitment Consultant at Hudson Global Resources

January 2004 - November 2004 (11 months)

Executive search and recruitment specifically with a Sales and Marketing focus.

National Business Development Manager at Biniris

September 2001 - December 2003 (2 years 4 months)

Senior Executive Business Development position.

1 recommendation available upon request

Regional Manager at Spotless

April 1994 - September 2001 (7 years 6 months)

Executive leadership position in the facilities services sector.

Regional Manager at P&O Services

1994 - 2001 (7 years)

Executive leadership position in the facilities services sector.

Skills & Expertise

Professional Services
Marketing Communications
Supply Chain
Lead Generation

Strategy
Telecommunications
Building Relationships
Executive Search

Strategic Partnerships
Consulting
Headhunt
Human Resources
Recruiting
Management
HR Consulting
Start-ups
Business Networking
Screening Resumes
Executive Coaching
Operations Management
Business Development
Contract Recruitment
Outsourcing
Search
Talent Acquisition
Team Building
Employer Branding
Guitarist
Professional Experience

Thought Leadership
Staff Management
Networking
Sourcing
Executive Management
Leadership
Technical Recruiting
Temporary Staffing
New Business Development
Account Management
Internet Recruiting
Recruitment Advertising
Coaching
Permanent Placement
Temporary Placement
CRM
Personnel Management
Talent Management
Graduate Recruitment
Marketing
Relationship Management

Education

Queensland University of Technology
MBA, Business, 2001 - 2003
2 recommendations available upon request

Griffith University
B Com, Marketing and Human Resources Management, 1986 - 1993

Brisbane Grammar School
HSC, 1981 - 1985

You'll note that I wanted to SEO my profile for both "executive search" and "career coach", and you can see how many times both of these phrases occur in my profile.

Now, if someone were to do a search on either "executive search" or "career coach" in "Brisbane" my profile would come up as one of the first on the relevant search.

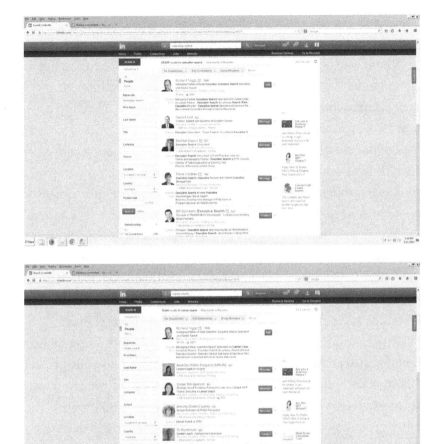

To get this right will require you to play around with your profile a lot, and then test keyword searches to see whether your changes have resulted in a higher ranking on a LinkedIn search for those particular keywords.

So that you don't look like a complete weirdo to those people you are connected to (especially your boss/colleagues if you are currently employed), you want to make sure that you turn off the function that alerts your connections when you alter your profile.

The way to do this is to go into your "Accounts and Settings"; then "Privacy and Settings"; and then under "Privacy Controls", turn off your "activity broadcasts". This way you can muck around to your heart's content, and no one will be the wiser. Make a few changes, check your search ranking, make a few more, and check again, until such time as you are number one or at least in the top ten, when someone does a keyword search on your most important attributes.

One thing to note is that if you were to for example write into your profile, *"civil engineer civil engineer civil engineer civil engineer..."* over and over again, if the LinkedIn authorities discover this, it is highly likely they will delete your profile completely because it is obvious you are trying to scam the system. So use some intelligence here and add your keywords as much as is appropriate without being over the top.

There are a few other things to do, which will both increase your ranking in searches plus add even more credibility to your profile. Firstly, make sure you join as many relevant groups as you are able to (at the time of writing this book you can join up to 50 groups). The more groups you are in, the better this affects your search ranking (this has something to do with the search algorithms that LinkedIn uses, but don't ask me what that means as I don't really have a clue!).

Make sure the groups you join are relevant to your career and professional interests – university alumni, professional bodies, geographical locations (such as Brisbane Professionals, a group I own that now has over 6,200 members). Don't join the "I love puppies", "single and desperate", "knitters anonymous" style groups because they certainly won't add to your professional credibility. Join 50 relevant professional groups that make you look connected, interested and interesting.

Then try and get as many "Recommendations" as you possibly can. This is where you invite one of your connections to write an endorsement about you and why you are great at your job. A great way to do this is the old, "I'll scratch your back if you scratch mine" philosophy. You recommend your colleagues, clients, friends etc. and ask them to do the same in return. A profile with lots of recommendations again ranks higher in searches, plus makes you look more credible when potential employers view your profile.

The last thing is a fairly recent addition to LinkedIn being "Skills and Endorsements". If you are a regular LinkedIn user, you will have noticed you are now getting emails saying things like "John Smith has endorsed you for Project Management", for example. I currently have 433 endorsements for "executive search", many of which are from people I have never even met!

Up until recently I thought this feature was a load of rubbish and paid it no heed. However I have come to understand that once again, the number of endorsements you have influences your search rankings, so the more the better.

Another interesting thing about using endorsements is using them as a way of letting people know you have been thinking of them. It's a simple way of offering a compliment, as long as it is sincere and to someone you actually know (in my opinion). Whilst I never used to endorse people, now I make it a habit that whenever I look at the profile of someone I know, I take the time to endorse a few of their skills. It's a nice thing to do, they get an email saying I have done it which is an easy way to show them I have been thinking of them positively, and it actually helps to improve their profile. A great win/win, so I definitely recommend doing it.

If you have a well written LinkedIn profile, that clearly articulates your professional history and qualifications, that's a great start. Add in your key achievements and transferable skills, and your profile is really starting to look good. Search Engine Optimise your keywords, join lots of groups, get lots of recommendations and endorsements, and now your LinkedIn profile is AWESOME, and you will definitely stand out from the crowd as a highly desirable candidate (at least in writing).

In this chapter, I've shown you that:

- Zero Moments of Truth mean that you are being viewed and judged well before an employer even sees your CV or meets with you

- Your LinkedIn profile is the CV of the future, and you need to ensure not only that the content is of an excellent standard, but also that it is Search Engine Optimised to get the greatest chance of being seen by recruiters and prospective employers

- LinkedIn Recommendations and Endorsements are also key to being seen and perceived as a top executive candidate.

CASE STUDY #3:

How Tania, a Senior Organisational Development Manager, Grew Her LinkedIn Connections and Confidence

Summary:

I was previously a Senior Organisational Development Manager within the Education Sector, but a recent relocation left me without a new job. I have a difficult time promoting myself because I feel uncomfortable sharing the achievements and experience that I have with others. Unfortunately, this has made it more difficult for me to find a job that I desire. I attended the seminar by Richard Triggs, "Always Stand Out," and learned more about LinkedIn, a site that I was already using to seek a new job. While I learned a lot of important skills that have helped me to grow my LinkedIn connections, I also was able to improve my confidence level. My improved confidence is helping me in my job search, and I am enjoying many benefits from the information I learned at the seminar.

The Problem:

Unlike many other individuals, I did not lose my job due to the economy or due to being fired. However, a relocation did leave me without a job. I previously worked as a Senior Organisational Development Manager within the Education Sector and I have plenty of excellent skills that should be transferable to another company.

My big problem is getting out there and showing what I can offer a company. My shyness and modesty often get in my way as I search for a job. I am not a big fan of sharing my previous achievements with others, since I do not want to feel like I am bragging.

My shyness has also kept me from growing my network on LinkedIn. I am shy about reaching out to other people, which is important when trying to build connections on a professional networking site. I was not accepting endorsements that were offered to me on LinkedIn, which also was hurting my job seeking results. I was behind on trends within my industry as well.

Since my confidence levels were low, I was not able to get out there and tell employers why they should hire me. I needed to increase my confidence and start sharing my achievements and experience with others to finally get the job that I needed.

The Solution:

I attended the "Always Stand Out" seminar and I learned so much that I have put into practice. Once I had some great information to guide me, I started making big changes on LinkedIn that offered some excellent results. For example, I updated my profile to make it stand out more to potential employers. Richard provided information on how the LinkedIn search engine works, and with that in mind, I went over the transferable skills and specialties that I had listed on my profile. I made sure that every part of my profile was optimised for the search engines to bring more views to my LinkedIn profile page.

I also learned about the people search function that comes with LinkedIn. I started using that function to find other individuals to connect with. For example, I have found other consultants and academics that work in similar areas, which has provided me with some valuable connections. I have also been connecting with previous colleagues on LinkedIn, which has proven helpful as well.

In the past, I had refused endorsements from other individuals, since I did not believe this was an authentic function provided by LinkedIn. However, I learned from Richard that endorsements really help to improve overall visibility to recruiters on LinkedIn. I now accept all the endorsements that I receive and realise that they help to show off my abilities and talents as I search for a new job.

The Results:

Since I began optimising my profile, using the LinkedIn people search feature and accepting endorsements, I have seen significant growth. My LinkedIn connections have already grown by more than 100 people, which surprised me. My goal is to hit at least 500 connections on LinkedIn by the end of this year. The connections I have made are valuable connections too, which is important to me.

Not only have I seen my LinkedIn network grow, but I have also improved my confidence levels. I still feel a bit shy and uncomfortable about promoting myself as an Australian expert. However, I have realised that I must promote my achievements and experience if I am going to find a new job. I am learning to step out of my comfort zone, and I now have the confidence to do so, which is improving my results as I continue to search for the right job after relocating.

I feel that I learned so much by attending the seminar with Richard Triggs. I'm continuing my job search, but I'm so proud that my network is growing and it is exciting to see my confidence growing as well.

4

CONNECTING DIRECTLY WITH YOUR EMPLOYERS OF CHOICE

Where are we up to now? You have worked out your job/s of choice (same job/same industry; same job/different industry; different job/ same industry; different job/different industry). You have an excellent LinkedIn profile (and CV), which clearly articulates your key achievements and transferable skills. You have Optimised your LinkedIn profile to ensure you come up at or near the top of the list when a recruiter is doing keyword searches on your specific skill set (as it pertains to your job of choice).

This is where it gets exciting. What you are going to do now is to reach out directly to your employers of choice, in order to get in front of them before they even know they need you. You are going to sell yourself on your key achievements and transferable skills (yes, I keep reemphasizing this point because it is the basis of your value proposition). This is how you are going to uncover the hidden job market.

When job seekers meet with me, often one of the first things they say is that they don't know who their employers of choice are. When I ask them, it's not uncommon for the candidate to say, *"I really don't mind who I work for. It's not about the company; it's about the culture, the challenge and the opportunity"* etc. Of course, that goes without saying, however you have to start somewhere. When you say the company could be "big or small", "listed or privately owned", "national or local", "in no particular industry", and other equally unclear and vague parameters… well, as the expression goes, "how long's a piece of string?"

There are some easy ways to get much greater clarity around identifying your employer of choice, but first I want to talk about the Reticular Activating System (RAS). For those unfamiliar with your RAS, it's a part of your brain that acts as a filter, letting through important information whilst blocking other less important information.

Imagine you went through your day, and every piece of sensory information you picked up was brought to your conscious awareness. Every sight, sound, taste, touch, smell and even emotion. With all of the advertising, noise, and general mayhem going on, you would go into sensory overload. Your brain would probably actually explode (only joking, but you get my point).

The job of the RAS is to filter out all the "stuff" so that you only become actively conscious of what is important to you. The rest of the world is getting on with its business, however in the main you aren't taking much notice.

Just imagine you decide you want to buy a new car. In particular, you want to buy a bright red VW Golf. You go down to the dealership, take a test drive and grab a brochure to bring home. All of a sudden, everywhere you look you start to notice bright red VW Golfs.

Uncover the hidden job market

Suddenly it seems like you can't drive for five minutes without seeing one at the traffic lights, then one at the shopping centre carpark, and even in advertisements in the paper/on television and so on. The car you thought was so cool and unique now is literally appearing everywhere.

You have instructed your RAS (subconsciously) that this information is important to you. So now the RAS does a great job and starts bringing every sighting of a red VW Golf to your attention.

The red VW Golfs were always there; you simply did not notice them. This is important and extremely relevant for identifying your employers of choice. Likewise, you have now instructed your RAS that identifying employers of choice is important to you. Now every time you read the paper, watch TV, are talking to a friend, and so on, your RAS is going to be tracking and identifying information for you about potential employers of choice. Whereas previously you did these activities without noticing potentially relevant employer of choice information, now it is going to come to your attention.

The important thing to do is to make sure that you take note of this information. Doing this reinforces to your RAS, that the information is important to you, which will further accelerate the RAS doing its job even better. It's a bit like showing gratitude and giving thanks every time your pet performs well, to emphasise its good behaviour. Your dog returns the ball, you say "good dog". Your RAS identifies an employer of choice, you say "good RAS". Well, not really, but by taking note of the information and writing it down, you are essentially doing the same. Plus, you won't forget, which is an added bonus!

There is also a heap of great tools you can use more proactively to identify these companies. Firstly, you can find lists of companies, which is an easy way to get the ball rolling. Depending on where you live, there will be plenty of lists of local and or national companies around a range of criteria.

For example in Queensland Australia (where I live), Deloitte produces a report called the "Queensland ASX Index" which lists every ASX listed company that has its head office in Queensland, ranked from largest to smallest. There is also the Q400 Awards, which recognises each year the top 400 privately owned companies in Queensland. I am certain there will be equivalent lists relevant to where you live.

There are other lists like the BRW Fast 100, Smart Company Fast 50, multiple award lists for innovation, technology, employer of the year…the list of lists seems endless. All of these lists are a good way to get your thinking going.

Let's say that you identify a particular company as an employer of choice. You can then start to think, "If I like them then what other companies are like that?" Who works in the same industry, is a similar size, has a similar culture/supply chain model/etc.? Who are their suppliers, customers, and competitors? Suddenly your one identified company has become many.

Another way to identify companies is to get on LinkedIn and look at the profiles of those people that you respect and admire in your area of specialisation. Where have they worked previously? What seems to be the career path they followed?

Another way to identify companies is to get on LinkedIn and look at the profiles of those people that you respect and admire in your area of specialisation. Where have they worked previously? What seems to be the career path they followed across roles, employers and even industries? Could you replicate this in your own career to some degree? Lots of great ideas can come from this exercise.

You can also keep an eye on which companies are in the press for accomplishments and significant changes. Which companies have announced a major new initiative that you would like to be a part of? Which companies have announced a change of senior leadership (CEO and/or board) that seems exciting? Maybe if you like crisis management and major change programmes, then which companies seem in trouble and could use your help?

Finally, which companies are specifically advertising roles for new employees? This could be a sign they are growing, going through a period of disruption, or some other change is afoot. The specific role advertised might not be one you want or are suitable for, however it could indicate a potential appetite for your skill set too.

You now have your list of potential employers of choice. Hopefully it is long enough to provide sufficient scope for your job seeking activities, but not so long that you get confused and don't know where to start. Don't fall into the trap of "paralysis by analysis". If the list seems too long, then prioritise which companies are truly the ones you want to work for. You can always start on your B priorities if you exhaust the A list.

The next thing you are going to do is to research the specific individual within the target organisation that you would most likely report to, and that you are going to reach out to. For example, if you are a senior finance professional, then the most relevant person is probably the Chief Financial Officer (unless you actually want the CFO job in which case the relevant person is the CEO). If you are an executive supply chain manager, then perhaps the relevant person is the Chief Operating Officer. Essentially you are looking for the person you are most likely to report directly to, or to be part of their team.

Unless you are an HR professional, you do not want to
reach out in the first instance to the HR Manager or the
company's recruitment personnel. They are too busy
filling their actual vacancies, to spend time speculatively
investing in you.

One thing to note is that unless you are an HR professional, you do not want to reach out in the first instance to the HR Manager or the company's recruitment personnel. The reason for this is that the HR team typically have a tactical orientation. What I mean by this is that unless they have a current vacancy at the time you make contact, and that you seem well suited for (i.e. a round peg in a round hole), then you are unlikely to get any real consideration. They are too busy filling their actual vacancies, to spend time speculatively investing in you.

Another thing you would never do is ring the company switchboard and ask how to apply for a job. Typically you will get directed to the company's "Current Vacancies" webpage to submit your CV, and in most instances it will disappear into a black hole, never to be seen again.

On the other hand, the direct line manager will have a strategic orientation. They are not just thinking about their current vacancies, they are also always thinking about building the level of talent in their teams. They want their life to be easier; so if they can get great people around them, life is better. They are also building their "talent bench", so that when a vacancy comes up, they know who to call first. You want to be on that list. Again, this is the hidden job market.

Using the example of a senior finance professional job seeker, they have now researched their employers of choice to find the name of the CFO. This should be easily done simply by looking at the company's website and finding the link to the organisational structure/executive leadership team webpage. If this is not easily identifiable, then Google for example "Rio Tinto executive team" and you should get a hit that will take you directly there. Another alternative is to look through the company's annual report, or as a last resort get on LinkedIn and do an advanced person search.

You now have the name of the relevant client contact. Now you get onto LinkedIn and find that person, who in today's environment is probably at least 90 percent likely to have a current active LinkedIn profile. One way to check how much of a LinkedIn user they are, is to see how many connections they have and how detailed their profile is.

If they only have a couple of connections and their profile lacks any real detail, then probably they accepted a couple of invitations in the past, but don't look at LinkedIn and use the site much if at all. If this is the case, the coming strategy will still work, however instead of contacting them through LinkedIn you will need to call the company and ask for the person's email address. Sometimes you will be given it; other times you may be given their PA/EA's email address.

If the receptionist asks what you need it for, you can say it's for personal reasons, or if you are a bit cheeky (like me) then say something like, *"I'm calling from the CPA (certified practicing accountants association) and need to send Mr Smith an invitation to our black tie dinner"*. Something like that, relevant to their industry, and you should get the email address easily.

Let's assume that John Smith (your relevant contact) has a LinkedIn profile. This is fantastic because for the first time ever, using LinkedIn, you now have the opportunity to directly contact your potential employer of choice. Whereas in the past you needed to rely on a recruitment consultant, or someone in your network who may know the person, for an introduction, now you literally can connect with them directly and immediately.

You have a couple of options here. If you are paying a monthly fee for a LinkedIn Premium account, then this gives you a quota of Inmails you can send each month. An Inmail is good because when you send one it goes directly into the person's inbox (Outlook, Hotmail or whatever they use) versus only going into their LinkedIn inbox (depending on how they have their account set up). However for the typical LinkedIn user, Premium accounts are expensive, you don't get many Inmails (and you're going to be needing lots following my recommended strategy), and as such I don't think they are worth it.

The second option, and the one I recommend, is to send the person a connection request that you have personalised (connection requests, unlike Inmails, are free and virtually unlimited – as you will see below). Its important to note that if you send connection requests to people you don't actually know, and they take the time to flag you as being "unknown" to them, then LinkedIn can put a restriction on your account. The penalty is that from that point on you would only be allowed to invite people that you have an actual email address for. You don't want to have this restriction on your account, because it severely limits your ability to invite those people you may know but don't actually have email addresses for.

(As an aside, it is quite easy to get this restriction lifted. You just contact Customer Service through LinkedIn, admit you have been naughty and will never do it again, and then they lift the restriction. So getting restricted is not really that big a deal, however it can be a bit of a pain to go through the process of having it removed.)

(As another aside, LinkedIn limits the total number of invites you can send to 3000. I suppose this is a way of trying to restrict spamming of people's profiles to build a huge mailing list. So when you get to your quota of 3000 then you will not be able to send any more. However, once again if you contact Customer Service and let them know you use LinkedIn as a business tool, then they will keep allocating you more invites to use, in small batches, each time you use up your quota.)

> Never send the generic *"Hi John, I'd like to connect with you on LinkedIn"* note that is automatically generated. Personalise every one, even if it is to someone you know well.

My advice is to never send the generic *"Hi John, I'd like to connect with you on LinkedIn"* note that is automatically generated. Personalise every one, even if it is to someone you know well. It doesn't take more than a few seconds and makes the message far more meaningful and respectful. I probably get around 100 connection requests every month from random people on LinkedIn wanting to connect with me (God knows why a computer programmer in Bangalore would ever want to be my connection?) and I'd say only maybe one of these personalises their connection request message. It's weird that people value their quantity of connections over quality, however that's a whole other discussion.

Coming back to your strategy of connecting with your employer of choice, you are going to send a connection request, with a message that goes something like this:

> *"Hello John, we have not met before however you are part of my extended LinkedIn network. I'm a senior finance executive currently working for XYZ*. I'm starting to consider my next career move and would really appreciate the opportunity to buy you a coffee and get some advice. I've always regarded your*

company, XYZ*, as a potential employer of choice. I'd like to have a talk about my skill set and how I may be able to add value to your team. At the very least, I am sure based on the success of your career, you can probably give me some great ideas about what I should consider for my next career move. Please feel free to give me a call on 04** *** *** or reply to this message letting me know your availability. Otherwise I'll give you a follow up call in the next few days. Regards, Richard".

(Please note: this message is probably too long for a connection request, however use your own judgement and modify to suit your circumstances.)

John gets your connection request and assuming he reads it, he will appreciate the fact you have been honest that you have not met him before; that you are being proactive without being pushy; that you are complimenting both his organisation and his own career; and that you have finished with a call to action. This will encourage John to look at your own LinkedIn profile.

Of course, your LinkedIn profile is excellent, it clearly articulates your key achievements and transferable skills, and he wants to know more. John makes a judgement call in his own mind that you are "fair dinkum" and not a "tyre kicker" (two Australian expressions that basically mean your approach to him is legitimate and that you have the requisite skills and experience to justify contacting him in the first place).

Three potential things are going to happen from here:

1. John does not accept your LinkedIn connection request and deletes your message (hey, s**t happens and this is a numbers game. Don't be discouraged as you are still going to follow up with John anyway).

2. John accepts your connection request, however does not respond to your message (this happens in the majority of cases).

3. John accepts your request and replies to your message, either online or by telephone, to speak to you and potentially arrange to catch up (this is the best result).

As I mentioned earlier, I recently ran a workshop teaching senior executives how to do exactly what I am explaining here. I had 83 people in the room, ranging from CEOs and HRDs through to mid-level managers. I asked everyone in the room, *"Who either is or was in a leadership role and managing teams"* to put up their hand. Everyone did.

I then asked, if they received a message via LinkedIn like the one I have just described, and then after looking at the person's profile and seeing they were legitimate, whether they would have the meeting? 83 hands went up. Every single person in the room would have the meeting.

I finally asked, *"How many of you are actively sending messages like this out to your employers of choice currently?"* Not one hand went up. Not one single person was sending messages and requesting meetings, yet every single one of them said if they received such a message they would definitely have the meeting. Pretty crazy stuff, huh?

One person in the room had just exited his role as Human Resources Director of one of Australia's largest and most successful mining companies. I directly asked him in front of the group whether, if he received a message like the one I had described, from a senior mining executive, he would take the meeting. He said, *"Richard, I would take that meeting every day of the week"*. I asked him how often he got messages like this, and he said, *"virtually never"*.

Whether you are looking for a new job or not, it's always important to keep building your networks within and across industries, and the best way to do this is face to face, over a coffee meeting.

There are some important points to note here. Firstly, to me as an executive recruitment consultant and career coach, this strategy seems so basic I struggle to understand why everybody isn't doing it all the time, just as a matter of course. Whether you are looking for a new job or not, it's always important to keep building your networks within and across industries, and the best way to do this is face to face, over a coffee meeting. Yet it appears almost no one is doing this at all.

The executive line manager you have contacted wants to meet you (although they may not know it yet). They have looked at your profile and you appear, on paper at least, to be a potentially attractive new employee. You have taken the time to make a proactive direct approach – which no one else is doing. Plus, if they meet you, like you and hire you, they don't have to pay a recruitment fee. This potentially saves them tens of thousands of dollars. Why wouldn't they agree to have the meeting? At the very least, by meeting you, they are finding out some industry information/gossip; assuming you are a good candidate then they are building a talent bench for future opportunities; or the Holy Grail is that they see an immediate opportunity for you in their business and they offer you a job.

Let's step back for a moment and consider an alternative scenario. The CFO has a vacancy in his team. Maybe someone has resigned, retired or been terminated for poor performance. The first thing he does is think of who he knows that is available, has the required skills and would be a good culture fit. Assuming no one comes to mind, he may ask some of his peers, colleagues or team members who they know. Again, assuming no one is identified, he then goes to internal recruitment (or an external agency) and briefs them. This all takes time, is expensive, and has no guarantee of delivering a good result. It distracts him from his regular duties; he has to work harder to compensate for the vacant role (or his team does which could cause retention issues); and is quite frankly one more problem he just does not need!

> If you are waiting for the advertisement to appear for a vacancy before applying, then you are so far behind the eight ball, and competing with so many other candidates, it's no wonder that almost all jobs get filled before they get to the open market.

The recruiter finally gets the vacancy, they run through their own immediate network, then their database, and then they put up an advertisement for the role. Are you starting to see that if you are waiting for the advertisement to appear for a vacancy before applying, then you are so far behind the eight ball, and competing with so many other candidates, it's no wonder that almost all jobs get filled before they get to the open market?

Compare this to you reaching out directly to your employer of choice's most relevant executive line management contact. You get in front of them before they know they need you. Rather than being compared against potentially hundreds of other candidates for an advertised vacancy, you are being judged purely on your own key achievements and transferable skills. Your potential new boss is thinking to themselves, *"This person could add a lot of value to my team. They could replace Bill who is retiring/not performing/wanting to be promoted* into a more senior role. Maybe they could head that new initiative/project/ division I've been wanting to start."

Can you see how much easier and smarter it is for you to proactively and directly engage this way, rather than going through the traditional recruitment process of dealing with recruitment agencies and responding to job ads? I truly hope so for your sake, so that you can get a great job as quickly as possible.

Coming back to your direct approach, let's assume you have not heard back from John, the CFO you sent your message to via a LinkedIn connection request. Whether he accepted your connection or not, the next stage in this process is the same. A couple of days (maximum four) after sending your message, you are going to pick up the phone and call him.

GASP! "You mean I actually have to cold-call someone I don't know?" I hear you thinking now, as you start to sweat and stammer. Yes, my job hungry friend, you are going to pick up the phone and call someone you don't know (remembering of course that a stranger is just a friend you have not met yet). This is what separates the adults from the children ("men from the boys" being far too sexist an expression in today's politically correct society); it's the road less travelled, the hero's journey.

Once again, going back to my presentation of this material to the 83 senior executives, feedback from all attendees was that the material was great; the instructions clear and simple; and that it just made good sense. Two months later (at the time of writing), if I had to guess I would say that less than 20 percent have sent any LinkedIn messages; less than 10 percent have made a consistent practice of sending messages (perhaps five plus messages a week); and virtually none have picked up the phone.

One executive who came to the seminar had been the CEO of a government owned corporation (GOC), whose role had been made redundant due to the amalgamation of his organisation with another GOC approximately 18 months previously. During this 18-month period I had met with him about three times, always offering the same advice as I've just stated here. He then came to my workshop, and a couple of days later invited me for a coffee. He is still unemployed.

I asked him how many times in the last 18 months he had reached out to a "stranger" within a potential employer of choice asking for a meeting? His response was, "never". Here is a guy who managed an organisation employing hundreds of people, with an operating budget of hundreds of millions of dollars, yet he could not find it in himself to send an email, let alone pick up the phone to call a potential future employer.

I asked him what was holding him back. He said, *"Richard, I guess I'm a bit old fashioned and I just expect that these people should want to call me".*

My response, *"So how's that working out for you?"* Needless to say, not very well considering 18 months later he's still looking for a job and starting to consider some serious compromises in terms of salary, position and even location to get the "advertised" vacancy. This certainly would not be my preferred strategy, but hey, whatever gets you through the night, right?

So you are going to follow up your LinkedIn message with a phone call. You call the company switchboard and ask to speak to John Smith (the CFO, remember?). If the receptionist asks what for you tell them it's a personal call. If you then get put through to John, that's a great result. If you get his voicemail, leave a message. Yes, I know this probably contradicts all the sales training that says never leave a message, but you're not a salesperson. You're a professional making a call to another professional. Leave all the stupid sales gimmicks to others, and leave a message – which you will follow up again the next day.

If you get put through to John's EA, explain you are following up on a message you sent to John via LinkedIn. Be honest and respectful. Remember, John wants to take your call, and he wants to meet you, because you are AWESOME.

When you eventually get to speak to John, the script goes something like this:

> *"Hello John, it's Richard Triggs calling. I'm following up on a message I sent you via LinkedIn a couple of days ago. Did you receive it? (YES) Great, well as it said, I'd really appreciate the opportunity to catch up with you for 30 minutes to get some career advice. When would it suit you to meet? I'm happy to come to your office or buy you a coffee somewhere convenient? ... Great, thanks very much and I look forward to meeting you then. Would you like me to send you a calendar invite?"*

Of course, John may not have seen your message, in which case he'll want to either check his LinkedIn inbox whilst you are on the phone or ask you to call back. He may be too busy to meet you right now, and ask for you to follow up in the future. He may say that he has no suitable vacancies in his team. In a nutshell, he is trying to get you off the line and get on with the rest of his day. Which is absolutely fine, and something that you and I have probably also done hundreds of times when we are busy with other things. So don't take it personally, and don't hold it against him.

If you don't get the meeting straight away, there's a (sales) rule of thumb that says it generally takes six "touches" to get a meeting. If it happens sooner, that's a bonus.

- Touch one was your original LinkedIn message.

- Touch two is your phone call (actually speaking, not just leaving a message).

- Touch three is sending John an email after you speak, thanking him for his time on the phone and letting him know you will follow up again in a month (or whatever timeframe he says but definitely not longer than a month, even if he says three months).

- Touch four is one month later, when you make the follow up call.

  > *"Hi John, it's Richard Triggs. We spoke about a month ago, when I asked if you could spare me 30 minutes to offer me some advice about my next career move. I'm just following up to see whether you might have some time available over the next couple of weeks?"*

- If you still don't get the meeting, touch five is the email you send him after the call, again thanking him for his time and stating you will follow up again in a month.

- Touch six is when you call again in a month.

By this stage, John is thinking that you have been very professional and diligent in following up via email and phone calls exactly as you said you would, and you have been proactive without being pushy. He's also going to be thinking, "If I don't meet this guy, he's never going to let up." So typically, by touch number six you have your meeting.

(As an aside, I recently heard a statistic that before making a serious buying decision, a buyer typically has eleven "touches" with the product/service, and spends seven hours considering their purchase decision. This is why online marketing is now providing lots of videos, testimonials and other content on their websites/YouTube etc. so that the consumer can easily access enough content to rack up the requisite seven hours' experience before buying. It goes back to the Zero Moment of Truth (ZMOT) principle that I mentioned earlier.

When I heard this statistic, it made immediate common sense to me in relation to recruitment and certainly applies to the process I am outlining in this book. As you are targeting the hidden job market, it is particularly important not to rush this process. You want the hiring manager to have their seven hours of "content" before making a buying decision. Trying to rush the process could easily end up derailing it.

Eleven contacts would include your initial email/s and phone call/s, coffee meeting/s, formal interview/s, psychometric testing etc. So relax, let things take their natural course, and if possible try to extend the process to seven plus hours, rather than doing what would seem more logical and rush to a hire/don't hire decision. Interesting food for thought.)

Of course, John could also be completely rude to you, in which case you'll just never get the meeting. Which is OK too, because it's all a numbers game, you are going to be emailing and calling lots of potential employers, not just John, and because don't forget, you're AWESOME.

Now you've finally got your meeting. It's taken a lot of hard work and perseverance, plus you've probably been pushed at least a bit out of your comfort zone. So whatever you do, don't blow it! Make sure you prepare well. If you fail to plan, you plan to fail.

Remember, this is not a job interview. It's just a meet and greet. The goal of this meeting is purely to get another meeting. So play it cool, don't act desperate, but at the same time be sure to put your best foot forward.

Many of the points you'll want to consider in preparing for this meeting are the same as when preparing for an actual interview. So rather than double up, remember to refer back to what I am about to say here, when you read the chapters later about interview technique:

1. Print out a copy of the person's LinkedIn profile. Google search their name to see what else you can find out about them (maybe they run marathons, play in a band or are a photographer, for example). Also print out some relevant pages from their company website and highlight some key points. When you meet, put these pieces of highlighted paper on the table in front of you. The person you are meeting with will notice the highlights and immediately appreciate the fact you have taken some time to prepare. Of course make sure you take a copy of your CV.

2. When in doubt, always dress as you would for an interview (even if its only the first coffee meeting) rather than down. It's much easier to take off a suit jacket and tie if you get there and the other person is dressed more causally, rather than be embarrassed because you are clearly underdressed for the meeting. They say you can tell the quality of a person by the quality of their shoes, so it goes without saying to polish your shoes, iron your shirt, brush your hair... you get the drill.

3. Never, ever disparage the company you are working for or raise any "dirty laundry" in this meeting or during any job interview. If your current boss is terrible, the company you are working for is hopeless, or your colleagues are a total pack of mongrels, keep this information to yourself. Remain positive and optimistic. Just say things like, *"it's time for a change/I feel I have more to contribute than I currently have the opportunity to do/I am*

looking for new challenges etc." By all means complain to your family and friends, but keep that stuff to yourself when meeting a prospective employer.

4. Remember that the point of this meeting is only to get to the next meeting. So keep the conversation reasonably low-key and don't oversell yourself. Ask lots of questions, give an appropriate amount of flattery (without being over the top), offer some examples of what you have done when it's suitable to do so, and make sure you close with a call to action. *"What do we need to do to progress this conversation/who else should I meet with to explore opportunities with your company/which other firms would you advise me to contact and can I say you referred me/etc.?"*

5. Always follow up with a thank you note. They will probably give you a business card, so you'll have their mailing address. Take the time to send a hand-written thank you card. The person's time is valuable, so even if there is no further opportunity for a role with their organisation, at least show appreciation for the fact they met with you.

6. Always follow up on any suggestions and/or instructions they give you. Make sure you keep them in the loop by CCing them on any emails you send and letting them know each time you achieve an outcome that was based on their advice. This person could still have a powerful influence on a future hiring decision. They could even become an impromptu, off-the-record referee, so you want to keep them on side as an advocate. Who knows, maybe the following week they are out cycling with their mates, or having a beer after an industry presentation, and someone says they need somebody just like you. You definitely want the person you met with to think

immediately of you and offer your name as a potential candidate. The only way to stay front of mind is to remain in regular and respectful contact.

Now you may think that what I have just described makes complete common sense, but let me tell you, virtually no one does all of the above let alone does it well. Yet if you just follow the above instructions, you will definitely stand out as an excellent potential employee for anyone you have the opportunity to get in front of.

In this chapter, you have learned that:
- Reaching out directly to your employers of choice is the greatest way to accelerate your job search process
- Your brain's Reticular Activating System can be switched on to assist you in identifying your potential employers of choice
- Using LinkedIn to connect and arrange meetings with key contacts within those employers is extremely easy to do
- Good preparation for these initial meetings will ensure the best chance of converting into actual opportunities for employment.

CASE STUDY #4:

How Sarah, an Environmental Manager, was Contacted Via a LinkedIn Inmail and Landed Her New Job

Summary:

An environmental manager, I found myself coming to the end of a 12-month work contract. Unfortunately, I realised that the job market was quite grim for senior managers, so I was not quite sure where I would turn once that 12-month contract ran out. Since I realised how difficult it would be for me to find a job in the current job market, I turned to Richard Triggs and his "Always Stand Out" seminar. I thought that his seminar would provide me with helpful advice I could use to secure a good job so I did not end up unemployed when my contract ran out. After the seminar, I took his advice and did a massive update on my profile. I continued tweaking my profile to increase my search engine results and I ended up getting a message out of the blue on LinkedIn, which ultimately led me to a new job that kept me from ending up unemployed like many other senior managers today.

The Problem:

My main problem was the fact that my contract was about to run out. I knew that it was going to be tough to find work in a market filled with senior managers looking for jobs. I wanted to know what I could do to make sure I found a job that I could transition into once my contract was up.

The Solution:

Since I knew how the job market was, I heard about the "Always Stand Out" seminar and decided to attend. Attending the seminar with

Richard Triggs gave me some helpful advice that helped me to update my LinkedIn profile so it stood out.

After learning all the techniques for building a quality, optimised LinkedIn profile, I put those techniques to work. I did a massive update on my LinkedIn profile. First, I updated my introductory spiel, writing it in the first person. I also included important keywords that I knew would help me stand out in the search engines, including "Environmental Impact Statement" and "Environmental Manager." I also started joining LinkedIn groups that were related to my industry and started jumping into the conversations.

After re-working my profile, I used the LinkedIn advance search function and searched for the terms, "Environmental Impact Statements" and "Environmental Manager." I found out where my profile was ranked and then I started tweaking my profile again. I continued using this method until my profile finally was at the very top of the first page for these search terms. I knew that would get my profile in front of individuals looking for people with my expertise.

The Results:

Out of the blue I ended up being contacted via a LinkedIn Inmail by an individual that had a position that was opening up with his company. He asked me to apply for the National/Principal Planner position that was going to be available. I was currently considering another position so I let him know that it would need to be a short application process. I had an interview that took a bit over an hour, which included quite a few technical questions. Then, I was asked to visit the head office in Newcastle for another interview. I had two interviews that included behavioural/reactionary questions and technical questions.

After several hours of interviews, I ended up landing the job of Principal Environmental Planner and I'm excited about my new opportunity. While I am still settling into my job, I'm excited about the opportunities in the future and I look forward to bringing new work into this organisation.

I am sure that it was my efforts on reworking my profile that resulted in my new job. With the techniques learned from Richard, I was able to continue tweaking my profile until I was at the very top of the search results for industry-specific search terms. It resulted in an unexpected message on LinkedIn, which ultimately resulted in me landing a great job.

5

HOW TO ACHIEVE THE BEST POSSIBLE OUTCOMES WORKING WITH RECRUITMENT CONSULTANTS

Even though this book is about how to access the hidden job market, there are still going to be times where you see a role advertised by a recruiter that you want to apply for. This means that you need to know how best to navigate your way through the often frustrating and unfulfilling process of working with third-party recruitment consultants.

Everyone has a horror story about previous dealings they have had with recruitment consultants. Believe me, I've heard them all. What you need to remember is that the recruitment industry requires no professional qualifications, there is no professional accreditation, and there are no barriers to entry. Quite simply, anyone can print a business card and then for all intents and purposes they are now a "professional" recruitment consultant.

In Australia, many of the larger recruitment companies seem to have a preference for employing English backpackers in their mid-20's, who with one week's training are now a Mining/Construction/

Accounting/etc. "specialists" with no prior industry knowledge at all (of course, I am generalising here). They have limited life experience, almost no professional experience, and certainly don't understand your value proposition and know how to sell you into a role. Most recruitment consultants I know I would not trust to walk my dog. I feel your pain!

> There are some very good recruitment consultants out there, who specialise in the industry you wish to work in, who know how to under-promise and over-deliver (they even know how to return phone calls), and therefore you want to know them and you want them to know you.

There are however some very good recruitment consultants out there, who specialise in the industry you wish to work in, who know how to under-promise and over-deliver (they even know how to return phone calls), and therefore you want to know them and you want them to know you. Once again, most job seekers have absolutely no idea how to build and maintain good relationships with good recruitment consultants. Follow the instructions to come and you will definitely find yourself in the top one percent of applicants.

To illustrate this example, let's say that I advertise a CEO role; one that looks interesting, is with a good company, and is generally a pretty sexy job. In this instance, I am probably going to get about 200 applications. That's a lot, right? Pretty hard to stand out from the pack, unless you do the following:

1.   Of the 200 applicants, how many do you think actually call me before submitting their application (my name is on the ad, after all)? Probably less than ten. The other 190 applicants

simply send in their resume and pray that they get a positive response.

Always ring the recruitment consultant before making an application. Make sure you prepare prior to the call, in order to ensure the best result. I should let you know that whenever I receive a call like this, I always let the caller know that I have someone with me and, *"I literally only have two minutes. How can I help you?"*

Here's an example of a bad call: *"Hi Richard, I see you are advertising for a CEO. (Yes – how can I help you?) Well, what can you tell me about the role?"*

At this point what I want to say would involve plenty of expletives about wasting my time when you can't even be bothered to read the ad. I pretty much do say that, minus the expletives.

Instead, read through the ad completely and prepare a couple of questions that show you have read it and are just looking for some clarification on a couple of points. The goal here is to start a relationship with me where you are already demonstrating yourself as a high quality applicant.

Here's an example of a better call: *"Hi Richard, my name is Mary Brown. I see you are advertising for a CEO. (Yes – how can I help you?) Well I notice that it is a national role – how much travel is required? / I see the company is in the property services sector – can you give me an indication of number of employees and turnover? / Can you tell me why the role has come about – did the previous CEO resign or has something else happened? / etc."*

Asking a couple of quality questions demonstrates you have read the ad and are genuinely interested. Once the recruiter answers your questions, you say something like, *"well on that basis I'll send through my CV and I look forward to meeting you soon"*. Do not start to go into your work history, suitability for the role, or try to get a meeting with the recruiter immediately – they are busy and that makes you look desperate.

2. Send in your application, making reference to the fact you have already spoken to the recruiter on the phone. Make sure you spell their name correctly; it's written on the ad (this is a pet peeve of mine) and don't write "To Whom It May Concern". Make sure your CV is tailored to the role you are actually applying for, and of course, make sure it clearly articulates your relevant key achievements and transferable skills (I don't care what you look like, so no photo please. I also don't care that you love cooking and romantic walks on the beach. Professional and relevant information only, thanks).

   When I receive 200 applications, I am at best going to give a cursory skim read of each CV to look for relevant job matching criteria. With that many applications, at this point I am looking for reasons to exclude an applicant rather than include them, simply to make my life easier. However when I see your application and recall our conversation, I am instinctively going to give you preferential consideration. In fact I may even go out of my way to look out for your application. This is why the phone call is so important.

   I appreciate that sometimes the recruitment consultant's name is not on the ad; sometimes they don't take your call; and more often than not they don't return your messages (as I said above, I've heard it all before). So just do your best, persevere and if you don't get to speak to them but you're still keen on the job, submit your CV regardless.

3. A couple of days later follow me up with a phone call. Something like this: *"Hi Richard, it's Mary Brown. I spoke to you a couple of days ago about the CEO role you are currently recruiting. (Yes – how can I help you?) I'm just following up to make sure you received my application and to ask when you expect to be shortlisting for interview? (Yes, your application is here and I'll be shortlisting by Friday.) Great thanks for your time. I look forward to hearing from you".*

   By this stage I like Mary Brown. She has shown that she is professional, has a genuine interest in the role, and has been proactive without being pushy. I am definitely (even if it is only at a subconscious level) going to give her application some preferential consideration. So, definitely make the call to follow up on your application. At this point, even leaving a phone message to say so is fine, and better than probably 98 percent of other applicants who never do this.

4. Even having made the initial call, followed up with a strong CV, and then made a follow up call, there is still a real possibility that you will not get an interview and will receive the good old TNT (thanks but no thanks) email. The one that says, *"Thanks for your application. There were much better qualified candidates so you aren't getting an interview. Tough luck and have a nice life"*, or words to this effect. We've all had them before; in fact I've received many myself.

   200 people have applied for my job. Assuming I choose to interview ten candidates, that means 190 people have received a TNT email. Of these 190 people, how many do you think call me to ask why, look for some advice for future applications, and potentially ask for a meeting? NONE. That's right, no one.

   This is simply crazy. The applicant has seen that I recruit CEO roles; they want a CEO role; they didn't get an interview for this role; but maybe I'll pick up another role they are more suited for. You would think that given this, they would at least want to speak to me on the phone, and preferably have a face-to-face meeting.

Remember I said earlier that TNT letters are your friends? This is because it gives you an excellent opportunity to start your professional relationship with me. So, PICK UP THE PHONE!

"Hi Richard, I recently applied for the CEO role you advertised. I received an email saying I was unsuccessful in securing an interview. I'd really appreciate some feedback on what I could do in the future in order to get a better result." Then after getting some feedback, you say, "Richard, I see that you are recruiting the type of roles that I am genuinely interested in. I'd really appreciate the opportunity to buy you a coffee and get your advice about my job search" (What? A candidate offers to buy a recruitment consultant a cup of coffee? Spend $4? I can't believe it! Seriously, a four-dollar investment in your future is a pretty good investment, people.)

Now, the recruiter may not have the time to meet with you. That being the case, no problem, apply the six-touch principle as discussed earlier, and put them into your call cycle.

You want to meet me (or the relevant recruitment consultant. There's no point in meeting me if I don't recruit the roles you are interested in. We would just be wasting each other's time). The reason you want to meet me is because you want to get preferential treatment for the next role, and the one after that.

Let's say I meet with a client after I meet you, who is looking for a new CEO. When they describe the attributes they are looking for, they may not be exactly relevant for your background. However because you and I have met, and because I understand your key achievements and transferable skills, I may say something like this to the client:

"*You know, based on what you said you are looking for, I may have an excellent candidate named Mary Brown. On paper, she does not have the exact background you are looking for, but let me tell you about her key achievements and transferable skills... I think you should definitely consider her. In fact, why don't you meet her before you go to the open market?*" Wow, you have just potentially been leveraged into a role that you would probably never have gotten if you had just been a traditional applicant.

It's all about relationships; it's all about connection. Treat your recruitment consultant with respect, invest in the relationship, and you will definitely be favoured for future opportunities.

This scenario will never happen unless you have a direct face-to-face relationship with the recruitment consultant. You have been professional and proactive. After the coffee meeting, you have followed up regularly, without being pushy, and kept the recruitment consultant updated on your job seeking status.

It's all about relationships; it's all about connection. Treat your recruitment consultant with respect, invest in the relationship, and you will definitely be favoured for future opportunities.

Of course, all of this is on the basis that you actually are a good candidate and you are applying for roles that you are actually qualified to do. Nothing annoys recruitment consultants more than people applying for roles they are clearly not appropriate for, as if they have nothing better to do with their time. The lesson here is to be conscious of your capabilities and realistic in your expectations. You'll save yourself a lot of time by only applying for roles you have a realistic chance of getting.

One of the questions I am often asked is how many individual recruiters a job seeker should have a relationship with. The simple answer is as many as it takes to ensure you have the best access to opportunities, whilst also ensuring that you are protecting your positive personal brand.

It goes without saying that a good recruitment consultant will treat you with respect. They will return your calls and emails and fulfil the promises they make to you regarding actions they intend to take. They will ask your permission before representing you to organisations and they will absolutely treat anything you have told them with the appropriate confidentiality the information deserves. These criteria alone probably cut out about 80 percent of recruitment consultants you will deal with. You will probably end up with three or four consultants from different firms that you will want to speak with regularly and meet with occasionally.

Here are a couple of things to watch out for. Firstly, historically recruitment consultants made a lot of placements (and money) by "floating" candidates, or "showcasing talent". This is where the recruiter will present a candidate's CV to a client for a potential vacancy, versus for a specific current role. In essence, the recruiter says to the potential hiring organisation, *"I've got a great candidate. Do you want to meet her? If you meet her, like her and hire her, then you will pay me a fee"*.

Pre-LinkedIn, organisations had very limited access to candidates, so often they would have these meetings, make hiring decisions, and the recruiter would be paid for the introduction. Whilst still a "regrettable spend" (i.e. the client does not like to pay the recruiter – this is how recruiters became known as "body shoppers"), the client often had no choice so they would accept the CV from the recruiter and have the meeting.

LinkedIn has changed all that. Now the client will probably say, *"I've got no current need for the candidate you are representing, and if I did then I'd (or my internal recruitment team would) just find her on LinkedIn myself. So thanks but no thanks".*

If a recruitment consultant asks if they can represent you to a specific firm, then you need to clarify with them that it is for an actual, real vacancy that they have been briefed on.

My advice to you is that if a recruitment consultant asks if they can represent you to a specific firm, then you need to clarify with them that it is for an actual, real vacancy that they have been briefed on. If it is just on the basis that the recruiter "knows" the client and "believes" they may have a "potential" requirement, then say no. You would be much better to approach this organisation directly (following the instructions I provided earlier) than to let the recruiter represent you. After all, if the organisation can get you for free, then why would they want to pay a recruiter a fee?

Secondly, often if you speak with a recruitment consultant, they will ask you what other roles you are currently considering/being interviewed for. If you don't know and trust that consultant, then DON'T tell them. Many recruiters use this question as a fishing expedition, and once you tell them then they will try to "cut your lunch".

For example, let's say you told the recruiter that you were at first round interview with ABC Company for a Group Accountant role. The recruiter could (I am certainly not saying every recruiter is this unethical) contact ABC Company and say, *"I hear you are currently recruiting for a Group Accountant? I have some excellent candidates I'd like to present to you on a contingent basis"* (i.e. the recruiter only gets paid if their candidate gets the job).

The recruiter then presents candidates other than you (because they won't get a fee if you get the job), increasing your competition for the role. If the recruiter is particularly unethical, they could even disparage you as a candidate in order to ensure their candidates get preferential treatment. You may think this sounds far fetched, but I was actually instructed to do this by my boss when I first started working in the recruitment industry. We did not work together for very long.

The simple solution is that when asked the question about what other roles you are currently being interviewed for, say something like, *"I have a few other irons in the fire however I am definitely very interested in the role I am speaking to you about"*, and leave it at that. If you have known the recruiter for a while and have developed a good level of trust, then you can be more explicit than that. Just use your own judgement and don't allow yourself to be bullied.

Remember that if a recruitment consultant places you, then depending on your level of salary they will make a large placement fee and earn a large commission. It is in their interest to treat you with respect, especially if you are a particularly good candidate. One of my old teammates used to call these candidates "money on legs". So demand respect, and if you don't get it, there are plenty of other better and more respectful recruiters out there.

When I first came into the recruitment industry, I quickly realised that if I wanted to be better than nine out of ten recruitment consultants I only needed to do one thing – return people's phone calls. It still amazes me that over ten years later, I still get complimented regularly by candidates (often very senior people even CEOs) for simply returning their phone calls. I live by the motto that "today's candidate is tomorrow's client" yet I know the vast majority of my competitors may pay this philosophy lip service, but they don't actually live it day by day through doing the simple things like returning calls and emails in a timely manner.

In this chapter, you have identified that:

- Having a proper plan for dealing with recruitment consultants will maximise your success in building good relationships
- You need to invest in these relationships to ensure you get priority access and consideration for the roles you are attracted to
- Good recruitment consultants will treat you with respect and likewise invest in and support your job search.

CASE STUDY #5:

How Simon, an Allied Health Industry CEO, Used LinkedIn Emails to Land Three Quality Job Offers

Summary:

I spent three years as the CEO of a privately owned, high growth Allied Health company, but ended up taking a voluntary redundancy. This resulted in my need to start searching for a new job. As I started my job search, I quickly found that limited opportunities were being advertised. When I applied for a job, sometimes I received no results, sometimes I was able to land an interview, but in the end, I had no success landing a job.

After attending an "Always Stand Out" seminar with Richard Triggs, I immediately started taking action, optimising my LinkedIn profile for search engines, updating my CV and working to grow my connections on LinkedIn. Ultimately, my work sending messages to offer my services as a consultant resulted in 30 meetings in a single month. Those meetings provided me with three different job offers. In the end, the results I saw from using Richard's techniques helped me to secure a CEO job with a privately-owned, health and safety consulting company.

The Problem:

The problem I was facing as I started looking for a new job was that I was always seeing inconsistent results in my job search. It was difficult finding opportunities in the first place, but when I found an opportunity and applied for it, the results varied so much that it was difficult to figure out what I might be doing wrong.

One of the problems I encountered was receiving no response when I applied for opportunities. This was especially frustrating because it is impossible to know why you are not being contacted or why you are not chosen for an interview. Another problem was that I would not receive interviews when I applied for roles that I knew I was qualified for. I had no idea why I was being turned away when I had exceptional qualifications that should have at least helped me land an interview.

In some cases, I did end up getting an interview after applying for an opportunity. After several interviews, I still did not enjoy success. A couple of times, I was told that I came in second for the role I had applied for, but I still received no information that helped me figure out what I needed to do to land a job for which I was qualified.

The Solution:

When I attended the "Always Stand Out" seminar, I received so much information that helped me as I searched for a new job opportunity. I learned how to optimise my profile on LinkedIn, I was provided with important tips for updating my CV and I learned how to start growing my number of connections on LinkedIn as well. My head was packed with information when I left Richard's seminar and I was determined to put all that information to good use.

I immediately started optimising my LinkedIn profile for the search engines. I added essential keywords that would grab the attention of individuals looking for people with my qualifications. I needed to be easy to find, so keywords helped me optimise my profile so I would stand out. I also made some changes to my CV, adding important keywords to my CV and ensuring that I provided information on my significant achievements and transferable skills. I started reaching out to other people in my industry on LinkedIn as well. I saw a significant growth in the number of LinkedIn connections I had in just a couple of weeks.

As I waited to land a full time role, I decided that I would begin offering my services as a consultant. I thought that this would be a great way to get my foot in the door, so I started to make use of my LinkedIn connections. I composed an email that showed my experience and expertise. I also requested a meeting with the individuals I contacted to discuss how I could help them deal with their current requirements. The following is the email I sent to approximately 300 of my direct LinkedIn connections:

Hi XXXX,

I thought I would reach out to you given we are connected on LinkedIn, to ask for your help please. I have recently stepped out of a full time executive role, and am now offering my services as a short-term interim executive. I'd be very interested in speaking with you about any current requirements you may have that I can assist with, and I would also appreciate you referring my details to anyone you know that I may be able to assist, in the following capacity:

Finance: *Finance and Analysis, preparation of board papers, interpretation and advice on financial performance*
Strategy and Planning: *Review and analysis of current position and advice on business direction, advice and support through the planning process*
Equity and Capital Raising: *Preparation and positioning of businesses for capital raising, development of Information Memoranda*
Change Management: *Guiding business through the process of preparation, communication and implementation of change*
Quality, OHS and Environment: *Development of manuals and documentation ready for certification to each of these standards*

Operational Efficiency Analysis: *Review of cost structures and operational activities to identify opportunities for improvement and efficiency*

Business Intelligence: *Creation and implementation of reporting structures and triggers for active response designed for significant business improvement*

Until recently, I was CEO of the XYZ Group, growing that organisation from 5 clinics to over 20 and more than tripling turnover in less than four years. Prior to this, I consulted to businesses from the very small up to large organisations including Rio Tinto on projects including business reengineering and restructuring, compliance and documentation, financial and reporting structures, grant writing and much else.

Quite simply, I am happy to become a very flexible resource that you can use for any finance/general management/project related work, whether it be a one day engagement, short-term or long-term project. No job is too big or too small – I can tailor my services to suit your requirements.

Indicative rates are around $*** per day depending upon your requirements and agreed deliverables, however I am happy to negotiate an arrangement that is commercially reasonable to all parties.

Please feel free to give me a call or reply to this email letting me know when would be a good time to have an initial discussion. I am available immediately and I look forward to seeing how I can be of service.

Regards,
XXXX

The Results:

After I mailed out those 300 messages on LinkedIn, I quickly began to see the results of my boldness. From the 300 emails I was able to set up 30 coffee meetings within 30 days. That was a significant improvement on my previous experiences searching for a new job. Not all of those meetings panned out for me, but I did end up being offered three different full-time job opportunities with several different interesting organisations.

Ultimately, one of those meetings turned into a job as a CEO. I secured a 12-month contract working as the CEO of a privately-owned, health and safety consulting company. Many of the strategies I used to get to this point were learned from Richard Triggs. I went from unsatisfactory, inconsistent results in my search to growing my network, setting up multiple meetings, ending up with several quality job offers and securing an excellent job that I'm very happy with today.

6

HOW TO STAY MOTIVATED DURING YOUR JOB SEARCH PROCESS

Let's take a bit of an interlude here and have a talk about motivation. Being a job seeker is hard work; it's almost a job in itself. You're going to be doing lots of tasks, getting out of your comfort zone, and probably at times your self-confidence and self-respect may take a bit of a beating. This will particularly be the case when you have to deal with recruiters (both external consultants and in-house) who may be a lot younger than you, don't understand your value proposition and often don't know how to communicate (except via Facebook – don't get me started!).

> It's important that you mentally prepare yourself for the fact that finding a new job may take a long time. A mindset that you are prepared to wait for the right job, rather than the first job, is a good place to start.

It's important that you mentally prepare yourself for the fact that finding a new job may take a long time. I regularly meet with candidates who initially have very high expectations about their new role (title, salary, location, etc.) yet after a couple of months start to compromise heavily on what they initially wanted. Whilst some compromise may be appropriate, the last thing you want to do is become desperate and accept a new role just because it's available, rather than actually being a good choice for you. A mindset that you are prepared to wait for the right job, rather than the first job, is a good place to start.

Seth Godin, in my opinion one of the best current writers on business, entrepreneurship and creativity, wrote a great short book called *The Dip* (2011, Hachette Digital). The premise of his book is that on the way to greatness, there are many obstacles to be overcome. It is a natural tendency that when most people come up against these obstacles, they quit. The time they are most likely to quit is during "the Dip", as illustrated here.

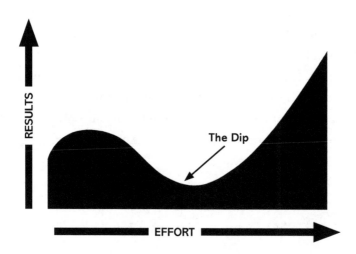

However, as you can see, the best results come after the Dip. As Godin writes, *"Extraordinary benefits accrue to the minority of people who are able to push just a tiny bit longer than most"*.

When I first saw this model, I could immediately see how it pertains to the job search process. Someone decides they want (or need if they have been made redundant/terminated) a new job. There is an initial flurry of activity – they register on Seek, apply for a few advertised roles, and meet a few recruitment consultants. They may get some interviews quickly. If they are lucky (or they are incredibly talented) then one of these interviews may turn into a job offer and they can then get on with their new job, and the rest of their lives.

However, what's more likely is that a few weeks in, they find out that they did not get the job they were interviewed for, the promises made by the recruitment consultant haven't been delivered upon (no big surprise here), and there just doesn't seem to be many jobs advertised that seem suitable or attractive. So the initial high levels of activity drop off, the job seeker becomes despondent, and for all intents and purposes they "quit" their job search process.

I'm going to suggest two strategies to help you to get through your Dip, to continue to take massive action, and to get the result you require (and deserve): a great new job with a great new employer.

One suggestion is quite practical; the other is a little more esoteric. You decide which one will work best for you, however I would personally recommend employing both concurrently.

The first strategy is to set yourself some clear and measureable Key Performance Indicators (KPIs) around your job search process. Like most things in life, the higher the level of activity, the quicker you'll achieve the desired results. The amount of time you can commit to your job search process will obviously be dependent on what else is going on in your life at the time. If you currently work fulltime then you will have less time to search for a new job than someone in between jobs. Regardless, my recommendation is to be optimistic about how much you can achieve and demand of yourself a high level of activity.

For example, you might say that each week you are going to:

- Send 20 LinkedIn connection requests to potential employers of choice;
- Follow up with 20 phone calls, ideally resulting in a minimum of 10 conversations;
- Arrange and have five face-to-face coffee meetings (or teleconferences if the person is interstate/overseas) with either potential employers or key persons of influence within your industry;
- Apply to five job advertisements; and/or
- Contact (or re-contact if you already know them) three recruitment consultants who specialise in your industry/skill set.

Break your KPIs down into daily activities, track your actual performance, and if you are falling behind then commit the time necessary to catch up. Most importantly, each time you achieve or exceed your KPIs for the day/week, give yourself a small reward.

For example, you might have recorded the next episode of your favourite television show. Make a commitment to yourself that once you have sent your 20 LinkedIn connection requests, you'll reward yourself by watching the recorded TV show (when I wrote this book I promised myself that as soon as I had finished this first rough draft, I would watch the next exciting instalment in *Game Of Thrones*). A reward like that will keep you on track plus will help you to make the commitment to sit in front of your computer (or telephone) and do the necessary work.

My second suggestion is a bit more out there. My recommendation is that each morning before you start your day, and each evening before you go to sleep, you spend five minutes meditating and vividly imagining your perfect end result.

It's said that the brain cannot differentiate between what is real and what is vividly imagined. Given that all the material that gets to your brain must travel through the five senses (sight, touch, sound, taste and smell) it seems to make sense that if you can create vivid enough imagery that encapsulates all of these senses, that's the same to the brain as experiencing the real thing.

We could get into a very deep and metaphysical conversation here about how thoughts become things and quantum mechanics, but for now let's just return to the earlier explanation of the Reticular Activating System (RAS). By doing a simple meditation practice, you are supercharging the programming of your RAS, and opportunities will be drawn to you even quicker than before. Words like synchronicity and coincidence (the co-inciding of events) have been used to describe this phenomenon. The opportunities were always there; it's just that your RAS did not bring them to your attention. Don't ask me how it works, just do it!

Write down what your perfect job with your employer of choice looks like, in as much detail as possible. Then include all of your five senses (I'll give an example in a minute) and also describe the emotions you will feel when you finally get that job. Work out a date that you would like to achieve the new job by.

Now imagine what that would look like as a movie, if you were the director. Here's an example of your movie script (you'll need to adapt to suit your own situation and ideal job/employer of choice):

I wake up and bounce out of bed, my sense of motivation in full swing as I begin to think about the first day at work. A new job is always a little tense, but the excitement easily overwhelms the nervousness as I begin to dress for the new job – the job of my dreams.

My favourite suit is hanging in the closet, ready for the first day. A fast shower and a small drop of my favourite cologne and I move into the bedroom to retrieve the suit. It's freshly dry cleaned, and a great new tie is just the perfect accompaniment. It fits to perfection and I leave the room knowing that I look my absolute best, important today more than any other day. Breakfast smells heavenly as I walk out of the bedroom door, well dressed, confident and smiling.

A great breakfast awaits me in the kitchen and I dig in, smiling at my family as they ask if I'm excited. I answer, yes of course. I take a last look in the mirror on the way out the door. The dog gives a little encouraging wag of his tail as if he too understands and I stand, rinse the plate in the sink and pull the kids close for a quick hug.

The car purrs to life and I glance at the mirror and back carefully out of the driveway, planning the day and making sure in my head that I didn't forget anything that I wanted to have with me today.

People at the new office are friendly, offering hellos and handshakes as I enter the building. The elevator to the office is full of people who smile and politely offer a good morning. It seems by far one of the friendliest places that I've worked, if you can call it work. Today I am doing what I love, living what I dreamed, watching my plans and hopes come to life.

The windows feature a gorgeous view and my friendly new boss shows me to my office, and I seat myself at the desk that already bears my name. No matter what tasks the day holds, *what chores hit the desktop, this is where I've dreamed of being...the life I wanted for my family and me starts right here, today. I'm holding it in the palm of my hand.*

Note the use of positive language and also that each of the five senses has been included – *see* the office, *hear* the introductions, *smell* and *taste* the breakfast, shake *(touch)* the people's hands. There's lots of positive emotion too.

Now what I want you to do is to write this story into a format that suits you, that describes your new job in detail and has the date by when you will have secured it. This could start with:

"By the 1st of September, 20**, I have started in my perfect new job. My role is based in Brisbane working for a multinational manufacturing company. I am the Sales Manager and I am earning at least $250,000 per year. I love my job, am really great at it, and I am excited about my future".

Print or write out your version on a piece of paper and stick it to your bathroom mirror so that every morning and night as you are brushing your teeth you can look up and read your statement. Close your eyes and vividly imagine the movie of your first day. Make it as real as possible, and add as much positive emotion as you possibly can.

When you have finished running this amazing movie through your mind, finish with the statement, *"All this or something greater".* Open your eyes, finish what you are doing, and get on with your day.

Sound corny? Maybe it is. But I guarantee if you do this exercise, you will be blown away with the results. There are hundreds of books written on the subjects of goal setting and visualisation. A couple of great ones are *Think and Grow Rich* by Napoleon Hill, and *You'll See It When You Believe It*, by Dr Wayne Dyer.

Regardless of how sceptical you are about all of this new age "mumbo-jumbo", do yourself a favour and suspend your disbelief for a while. Do it for a couple of minutes twice a day, in the privacy of your own bathroom. No one will ever know. When it works, thank the Universe (and me if you want to!) for a fantastic outcome. If it doesn't work (which won't happen unless you don't do it), then feel free to blame me – I can handle it!

By vividly imagining the perfect end result, coupled with a strong commitment to fulfilling your job search KPIs, you are ensuring you don't quit by getting stuck in the Dip. Don't forget – you're AWESOME.

In this chapter, I've shown you that:

- Maintaining your motivation during the job search process can be challenging, especially if you are not getting interviewed and/or offered roles you are excited about and feel you are qualified for

- Getting stuck in "the Dip" can cause candidates to quit their job search, or end up taking roles that are not ideally what they are looking for

- One way to maintain motivation is to set specific task goals and to celebrate the small "wins" in achieving these

- Another way is to clearly define your perfect job and when you want to have achieved it, and then visualise each day a "mental movie" of you achieving this perfect end result.

CASE STUDY #6:

How Shirley, a Technical Writer, Optimised Her LinkedIn Profile and Now Enjoys 500% More Profile Views

Summary:

I am a technical writer and I have spent a long time working as a freelancer. However, a need for better benefits led me to start looking for a full time job as a technical writer. I used online job sites to begin looking for a job, but no matter how many applications and resumes I submitted, it seemed like I was going nowhere. I kept supplementing my income with freelance jobs while I went without the benefits I needed.

A friend recommended the "Always Stand Out" seminar to me, so I went to check out what Richard Triggs had to offer. At the seminar, I learned more about optimising a LinkedIn profile and using all the tools provided to enjoy great results. I already had a LinkedIn page created, but after learning all the tips and suggestions from Richard, I went back and started implementing those tips. After just a few weeks, I saw my profile views increase by 500%.

The Problem:

The big problem I was facing was transitioning from working as a freelancer to finding a full time position. I did have experience working with freelance sites to find freelance jobs, but for some reason I could not carry that experience over to finding a full time job that offered benefits.

I began using online job sites to try to find a job. However, most of the jobs I found for technical writers were also freelance jobs, which is what I wanted to avoid. Anytime I found a good opportunity for a technical writer, I would submit my resume and a cover letter, yet I never heard back from anyone. It seemed I was continually putting time into something that was not working for me.

I heard that LinkedIn was a great networking tool, so I joined LinkedIn. I filled out my profile and tried making connections, but after a couple months, I still only had 25 connections and had no idea how to make the site work for me.

After several months of searching, I still had not found a full time job. I knew that there were technical writing jobs out there, but I just had a problem finding them and connecting with the right people.

The Solution:

After a friend suggested that I check out the "Always Stand Out" seminar by Richard Triggs, I was hesitant, but I really did not have anything to lose. It was obvious that what I was doing was not providing me with results. I attended the seminar to see if I could learn how I could secure a job by taking control of the job search process.

At the seminar, I learned so much about LinkedIn. I found out what an amazing tool it is and how important it can be when navigating the changing job market today. I realised that I was not using LinkedIn to its full potential. Richard offered information on how to optimise my LinkedIn profile to increase the number of profile views I received. He also gave tips on making my profile more attractive to both recruiters and employers. Richard emphasised being proactive, looking for potential employers of choice and going after a position with their company.

Empowered with all that information, I knew I had to implement everything I had learned. I started by using Richard's tips for optimising my profile, including important keywords and adding information that would make me stand out.

Next, I started using LinkedIn to research some employers I thought I would like to work with in the future. Then, I started reaching out to these companies, sending direct messages to them on LinkedIn and asking them to meet with me. I made sure that I sold myself, telling them I had something great to offer their company. I sent out many of these messages over time and did all the legwork to get meetings with these individuals.

The Results:

While it required a lot of work on my part, I was able to target my job seeking efforts and the work paid off. One of the big things I noticed was that optimising my LinkedIn profile really provided me with fast results. After I took the time to rework my profile, adding important keywords that grab the attention of recruiters and employers, I saw my profile views skyrocket. I had been averaging about 4–5 profile views a day before I reworked my profile. However, once I used Richard's advice and optimised my profile, I saw a 500% increase in profile views. After 2–3 weeks my profile was being viewed about 25 times a day.

While I sent out many messages to companies that I wanted to work with, ultimately it was not those messages that paid off in the end. It was actually the optimisation of my profile that brought me the results I wanted. I logged into LinkedIn one morning and had a message waiting from a large company that wanted to hire a full time, telecommuting technical writer – a job that was just perfect for me. A company recruiter came across my profile and thought I might be a great fit for the job. Three days later, I had an online Skype interview with the recruiter, which went well. A week later, I was offered the job. Now I still enjoy the benefits of working from home, but I have a full time position that comes with great benefits.

I had wasted so much time using ineffective techniques, but in less than 6 weeks after attending Richard's seminar, I finally had the job I wanted. Now I recommend the seminar to others who are having a difficult time finding a job in today's difficult and changing job market.

7

HOW TO PERFORM AT YOUR BEST DURING A JOB INTERVIEW

Whether through directly approaching your employers of choice, or through responding to a job advertisement, the time will come when you are actually going to be interviewed for a role. Just like when playing golf, you "drive for show and putt for dough", the job interview is where you have to perform at your best. Good preparation and learning some basic skills will massively improve your performance against the vast majority of candidates you are competing with.

Firstly, go back to my earlier section on how to prepare for a meeting with a prospective employer and remind yourself of the points there, as they are equally if not more relevant for your job interview. Find out the names of the people who will be interviewing you; print out their LinkedIn profiles plus company website information; and highlight some key information to show you have done your research. Read the annual report plus any other information you can find. If you know people familiar with the company interviewing you, then take the time to call them and ask some questions. All this will demonstrate you have done your homework, when you use this information appropriately during the interview process.

Always dress your best, be on time, and be respectful of all the people in the room (i.e. don't focus all your attention on the hiring manager, whilst disregarding the HR person sitting quietly in the corner – they may have a major influence on the final hiring decision).

Again, I am going to emphasise that you need to know and be able to clearly articulate your key achievements and transferable skills. Think back through your various roles. What are you most proud of? Where did you get the best results? How were these results appreciated by your boss/client/team/etc.? Really spend some time on this preparation. Ask your partner or friends to listen to you articulate this information and offer some critical feedback. Become really good at sharing your key achievements and transferable skills in an engaging, enjoyable and interesting manner. You'll see in a minute why this is so important.

Don't be humble (remember you are AWESOME), but also don't be a show-off, and definitely don't be dishonest. Be able to quantify your results (e.g. I improved profitability by x%; I delivered $x more revenue above budget; I reduced staff turnover by x%; etc.) and make sure that if you say it, then it can be confirmed by your referees as being true.

When you arrive for your interview (on time and well dressed), enter the meeting room and after the introductions, sit down, open your notebook, and put the highlighted printouts (LinkedIn profiles and company information) in plain sight. You're here for business and immediately the interviewers will take you more seriously.

One thing to always keep in mind is that most hiring managers (and even some HR managers) have no idea how to run a good interview. They have never been trained properly, so they just "wing it" as they go along. At best they may have prepared a few interview questions; at worst the hiring manager doesn't pay proper attention and may even check emails and take calls during the interview. So the more you can take control of the meeting and appear confident and collected, the better you will perform.

What I want you to do is to ask one killer question, as soon as it is appropriate to do so. This question is going to set the stage for you to show your brilliance; it's going to make you radically stand out from your competition; and it's also going to allow you to really, accurately determine if in fact you actually want the job on offer. This is the question you want to ask once you have exchanged pleasantries, and the interview has commenced in earnest.

Before we get there, a great way to open the conversation after introductions, is to say something like, "*Mary and Bill, I really appreciate the time you are taking to meet with me about this role. For you to leave this meeting today and feel really happy that you met with me, what would you like to achieve?*" Listen to their response and write it down in your open notebook. Ask some further exploratory questions around their responses, so that you are clear on their expectations. Keep this part of the discussion fairly light – don't make it seem like you are interviewing them. But definitely take the time to do this, as it will make you stand out, plus you'll use this information to close out the interview at the end.

Now, here comes the killer question. You need to pick your timing for when to use it, however you'll typically find the right opportunity fairly early in the conversation.

"Let's imagine I've been in the role for 12 months and we are about to sit down to do my performance review. For me to get 100 percent, having fulfilled your complete expectations, what would I have needed to have done in my first year of employment?"

Here goes:

> *"Mary and Bill, let's imagine I've been in the role for 12 months and we are about to sit down to do my performance review. For me to get 100 percent, having fulfilled your complete expectations, what would I have needed to have done in my first year of employment?"*

This question has been adapted from Lou Adler's excellent book *Hire With Your Head* (Wiley, 2007) where he uses a very similar approach to taking a brief from the client about the key deliverables they expect from the role he is recruiting for. He calls this approach "Performance Based Hiring". If you are a hiring manager, or even want to understand this approach from a candidate's perspective, then I highly recommend reading his book.

This is a great question, for a few different reasons. Firstly, most position descriptions are rubbish. They give no real idea of what the role requires; its unique nuances and specific deliverables. Most PDs are generic and written by someone who has had no training and often has no idea of what they actually want. Asking the interviewer this question early in the interview will enable you to get a much better understanding of the requirements of the role and how best to showcase yourself as a preferred candidate.

You may find that the hiring manager has difficulty in answering the question well. You may also find that if you are being interviewed by an internal HR/recruitment employee (and the hiring manager is not in the room), that they have no real idea of the actual key deliverables of the role. This is not to say they are incompetent, just that they have not been briefed properly. I can say from experience that this is often the case.

You need to be patient, and ask lots of further questions for clarification and to get sufficient information. Don't be satisfied with just one expected deliverable; ask *"what else would I have needed to achieve?"* multiple times if necessary, so that you end up with at least four, preferably six to eight key deliverables.

Another way to ask a similar question would be to say, *"Imagine I start in the role on Monday. What would the first 90 days look like? What would you want me to achieve in the first three months in order for you to feel completely confident that you have made an excellent hiring decision?"*

Whatever responses they offer, make sure you write these down. You are going to refer to these points often during the balance of the interview, so you want to make sure you remember them. Plus by writing them down, you are again demonstrating to the interviewer/s that you are professional and thorough, which are qualities they definitely want.

This is now your opportunity to be able to share your key achievements and transferable skills, by using these stated key deliverables of the role as talking points around which to share this information.

Let's use as an example, that you are being interviewed by the Chief Operating Officer for a General Manager role. You've asked the killer question to determine the key deliverables, and they say something like this:

> *"Our previous GM resigned a few months ago and this has left*
> *the business in a fairly poor state. Their team has not been*

performing well and retention is poor. We believe that the people are good and they want to do well, however they have been lacking good leadership and vision for some time. An early priority is to assess all of the team members for competency and commitment; then to build a shared vision for the team and get them re-engaged. If within 90 days you can report back to me that your team are now excited about the future and committed to achieving their goals and budgets, that would be a great result."

Compare this to another response:

"The business has been going through some challenging times. Whilst we were the market leader, new technology has allowed our competitors to be able to really reduce their costs and we are being consistently beaten on price. What we need you to do is to be able to quickly identify every opportunity we have to trim costs, whilst still ensuring we are delivering excellent service to our existing clients. A great result within 90 days would be to know clearly how we are going to reduce our operating costs by at least 25 percent within 12 months."

Or another response:

"The business has been going great. The team are performing really well and our clients love us. We see a great opportunity here to really leverage our existing business and grow our revenue by moving into some new markets, either geographically or by adding on some additional products and services. What we would like you to do in the first 90 days is meet with all of our major clients and then formulate a strategy for improving revenue and market share. Revenue growth of at least 10 percent in 12 months would be an excellent result."

Can you see how the same role of General Manager can have at least three completely different priorities? If you did not ask this question early, then there is a strong possibility you could start talking about your key achievements that are completely irrelevant to the requirements of the role. Asking for lots of clarity around expectations is going to ensure that you show your skills in the best possible light.

Now is the time for you to start talking about your key achievements as they pertain to the specific key deliverables. And if you have previously achieved those outcomes that they have described, but in a different environment/industry, then you talk about your transferable skills as they best compare to the explained key deliverables.

In essence, you use the key deliverables that they offer as the foundation points for describing what you have done previously, done well, and are motivated to do again. It creates the perfect platform for you to really demonstrate why you are the obvious best choice for the job.

> The key here is to describe in as much detail as possible the achievements you have had in your career that you are most proud of; those achievements that you would say most clearly demonstrate why you are excellent at your job.

The key here is to describe in as much detail as possible the achievements you have had in your career that you are most proud of; those achievements that you would say most clearly demonstrate why you are excellent at your job. Your stories are going to be like the targeting system on a guided missile, locked and loaded on the precise target, being an absolute demonstration through past experience that you can do exactly what the employer wants.

You'll blow the other candidates out of the water, and out of contention, when you do this well. Like everything else recommended in this book, practice makes perfect, so arrange a mock interview with a friend, or record yourself and listen back, honing your skills in delivering these great stories about your key achievements.

Of course, when they describe the key deliverables, you may decide that what they want is not what you are good at and/or not what you want to do. If this is the case, be upfront about it and withdraw from the role. You have saved both you and them a lot of time and energy wasted on furthering an interview process for a role that you don't actually want. You may also have saved yourself from potentially taking on a new job and then quickly realising that you are not happy. So even in this regard, asking for specific key deliverables is an essential thing to do.

I can tell you from my own experience of having interviewed literally thousands of executive candidates, and having participated in hundreds of interview panels in the employer/candidate interviews, almost no one ever asks these questions. So when you do, you are virtually guaranteed you will have a much better interview, leave a much better impression, and have a much better chance at securing the role.

As you get to the end of the interview, you will often be asked whether you have any further questions. This is not the time to be coy and say, "not really". You definitely want to ask some good quality questions, firstly to clarify any specific things you want to know, and also as a way of further demonstrating you have done your homework.

Maybe ask a question about the company's results or future strategy, that you have identified by reading their annual report. You may have heard something in the market that you would like to learn more about. A couple of well thought out questions, that further amplify your status as a preferred candidate, are sufficient.

Another good question is to refer to the person's LinkedIn profile and ask them something like, *"Mary, I see from your LinkedIn profile you joined this company just over three years ago. Why did you decide to join? What keeps you here? What do you like most about the company?"* etc. Good questions; they show you are interested in her as a person; and further elevate your status in her eyes.

At the end of the interview you want to finish by referring back to your original question and the points you wrote down. *"Mary and Bill, you said that for you to leave this meeting and feel really happy that you met with me, you would like to have achieved…? (Read from your notes) Are you happy that we achieved these outcomes? Is there anything else you would like to ask? Are there any questions you think I should have asked but didn't?"* In other words, are they happy with your performance?

This is a great way to end the interview, because you are demonstrating that you listened to what they wanted and have made your best efforts to deliver. You are showing that you have an honest appreciation for their time and a desire to meet their expectations. This is a very powerful thing to do and I'd be amazed if any of your competition has done this. Remember – you are AWESOME.

Close the interview with a call to action. Without being pushy, you could say something like, *"For me to have the best possible chance of getting this job, is there any further information or anything else you would like me to do post this interview?"* or, *"What's the next stage in this process? Who else will I need to meet?"*

After the interview, make sure you follow up with a hand-written thank you note, mailed to each of the interviewers, thanking them for their time and re-emphasising your strong interest in the role.

After the interview, make sure you follow up with a hand-written thank you note, mailed to each of the interviewers, thanking them for their time and re-emphasising your strong interest in the role. If you have been represented for the role by a recruitment consultant, make sure you call them promptly and offer good feedback. Thank them also for their efforts to date.

Then be patient, get on with your life, and wait for them to come back to you. Don't follow up prematurely and potentially present as being desperate. Be cool and trust that you have done a great job and allow things to naturally unfold from there.

> **In this chapter, you have learned:**
> - How to prepare for and perform at your best in job interviews
> - Powerful questions you can ask to ensure you can easily speak about your key achievements and transferable skills
> - How to close the interview with a call to action that will leave your interviewers thinking very positively about you as a preferred candidate.

CASE STUDY #7:

How John, a Freelance Graphic Designer, Targeted Potential Employees and Scored 40 Meetings

Summary:

Unfortunately, I am a graphic designer who found myself out of a job two years ago. The company I worked for had to cut back due to the poorly performing economy and I lost my job. I immediately started trying to find a new job. I used all the tricks I had used 10 years ago when I last applied for a job. No matter what I tried, I was not getting anywhere. I had heard about LinkedIn but did not think it was a serious site for finding a job.

A fellow graphic designer who was also searching for a job heard about Richard Triggs and his "Always Stand Out" seminar. We both attended and were astounded by what we did not know about searching for a job in this changing market. It quickly became evident that I was making big mistakes and those mistakes had kept me unemployed for two years. I learned from Richard how to use LinkedIn to approach people I wanted to work for, so I started using that technique. I targeted potential employers and with that strategy, I scored 40 different meetings. Two resulted in job offers and I am now employed with a company I actually love.

The Problem:

When I lost my job in 2012, my main problem was that I had not spent any time searching for a job for a decade. I'd worked with the same company for 10 years. Unfortunately, that was not enough to keep me from being laid off when the company started going downhill. Once I lost my job, I started going back to job seeking tricks that were old hat. Those tricks had worked a decade ago, but I was sadly misinformed on how to go about finding a new job today. I was frustrated because no matter how hard I was working to find a job, I was still unemployed. I was in serious financial trouble because of my job loss and it continued to get worse as the months went on.

During my two years being unemployed, I did hear a bit about LinkedIn from friends and family members. However, I dismissed LinkedIn. I really did not think that it would offer me any value. How could it help if all my old job seeking tricks were not providing results? I had no idea that LinkedIn was for professionals and definitely did not know about the incredible tools that the site has to offer.

The Solution:

I have a great friend who is also a graphic designer. He was also searching for a job, although he had only been without work for a few months. My friend heard about Richard Triggs and suggested that we attend the "Always Stand Out" seminar. I had never heard of Richard, but my job situation was so desperate at the time that I knew I had to do something. So, I tagged along with my friend to Richard's seminar.

At the seminar, I quickly learned how wrong I had been about LinkedIn. The seminar gave a nice overview of how LinkedIn worked and the benefits it has to offer professionals who are looking for a job. Just realising that such a great tool was available to me gave me a lot of hope. Apparently, I had been missing out on one of the best tools for job seekers.

After the seminar, I realised I had a lot of work to do, but I felt that this time my work would really pay off for me. I went home and started my own LinkedIn account that night. I spent a couple hours setting up my profile. The next day I worked on my profile more, using Richard's tips for optimising my profile using keywords that employers and recruiters would commonly use to find graphic designers. I used every tool available on my profile to make sure that I would stand out to companies that wanted to hire a graphic designer.

The next step I took was starting to contact potential employers. I began using LinkedIn to search for potential employers. I did not just choose any employer. I spent time doing some research, looking for companies that I thought I would really enjoy working for. I found out the individuals I should contact and started writing LinkedIn messages to those contacts asking if they would be willing to meet me to discuss how I could offer value to their company. I probably sent out a couple of hundred messages to people on LinkedIn. I was desperate and needed a job. I was willing to put in as much work as I needed to if it helped me to find a good job.

The Results:

At first, I thought I had taken another wrong turn. I did not receive any messages back for a couple weeks. I started feeling depressed. However, all of a sudden the messages started pouring in. Between LinkedIn messages and phone calls from individuals who I had messaged, I ended up setting up 40 meetings in the space of a month. That was incredible to me. I had not had any luck for two years and suddenly after a couple of weeks my schedule was packed with meetings with potential employers.

Not every meeting went well. Some companies did not offer me a job. Others offered me a job on terms that did not work for me. However, I kept going to those meetings. I kept sending out those messages. With continued effort on my part, one meeting finally paid off. I always added my phone number in the messages I sent out and one interested individual contacted me by phone to set up a meeting. When we met, I was excited about the company he was with. This was a company that was growing and I felt it would offer me a great opportunity. I did not hear anything back from the individual right away, but a week later I followed up with a phone call and I was offered the job.

After two long years being unemployed, I was so relieved to finally have a job. While I was dubious about how Richard's techniques would work, after a lot of hard work and many meetings, I have an excellent job. I know I would not have started using LinkedIn if I had not attended Richard's seminar. He introduced me to the power of LinkedIn and I was able to harness that power to land a graphic design job that I really enjoy.

8

HOW TO MANAGE THE JOB OFFER PROCESS

There are probably going to be a few more steps before you are offered the job. There may be a requirement for one or more further interviews with the same or different people making the hiring decision. You may even be required to write a report or give a presentation. Like everything else, make sure you are well prepared, do your best and be completely professional in your personal presentation and any written materials you may need to provide. A simple thing like poor grammar in a written report could make the difference between being offered and missing out on the job. If in doubt, get a friend or trusted colleague to proofread anything you are going to submit.

You may be asked to complete a psychometric test, especially for more senior roles. Take these tests very seriously as many clients may rely on the results for a hire/don't hire decision. Be well rested before the test, and if you are doing it from home make sure there are no distractions. Often these tests are timed so you want to make sure you complete as much of the test, as accurately as possible, within the time required. I have seen many excellent candidates miss out on an offer because they did not give the psychometric testing the respect it requires.

You will definitely be asked to provide at least two professional referees. The best referees are people you have directly reported to. Offering family friends or colleagues as referees could be perceived by your future employer as being that you have something to hide, so wherever possible use previous bosses as your preferred referees.

Never assume that just because you put someone down as a referee, they will in fact provide a good reference. Many times I have called a referee, who ends up providing negative information that costs the candidate the job. So always call anyone you wish to offer as a referee and ask his or her permission. Specifically ask, *"Are you happy for me to provide you as a referee? Is there anything that would stop you from giving me an excellent reference?"* If there is a potential issue, it's better to know in advance and either work it out, or don't offer them as a referee.

Tell your referee some information about the role you are being considered for, and why you are excited about it. Make sure you send them a thank you note, and keep them updated on the progress of your application. When you get the job, buy them a small gift (maybe a bottle of wine or some flowers) as a further thank you.

The last thing you want to do is get all the way to an offer, only then to decide you don't want the job after all. Even worse, you accept a job and then, quickly after starting, realise it is not meeting your expectations.

On the other side of the coin, by this stage you should have spent some quality time determining if this is actually a job that you really want; that will provide you with the work environment, challenges and opportunities that made you start looking in the first place. The last thing you want to do is get all the way to an offer, only then to decide you don't want the job after all. Even worse, you accept a job and then, quickly after starting, realise it is not meeting your expectations. That can have terrible consequences for both you and your new employer and you want to avoid this at all costs (mistakes do happen however and most people make at least one poor career decision in their lives – don't sweat it if you accept and then leave a role quickly. That's why employment contracts have probation periods, to protect both you and your new employer).

Lou Adler (in his excellent book *Hire With Your Head* which I mentioned earlier) presents an eleven-factor analysis for candidates to use when comparing a potential new role to their current one, plus any other alternatives. I think it's a great tool and one I use in my recruitment and career coaching business regularly, so here it is for your consideration:

1. Job match – Can you actually do the job you are being employed to do? Having asked what the key deliverables are, be honest with yourself as to whether you can actually achieve what is required and also that you will enjoy and feel motivated to do so.

2. Job stretch – Is there sufficient stretch in the role to keep you motivated and engaged? Will you be challenged and learn new things and/or develop new skills to fulfil the role, whilst still feeling confident that you can actually succeed?

3. Job Growth – What are the future opportunities within the role? Is there a clear career path, either through promotion to more senior roles, or through taking on bigger projects etc.?

4. Hiring Manager – Who is going to be your boss? Do you like and respect them? Do you think you will have a good working relationship? Do you think you will grow as a person under their leadership? There is a saying in the recruitment industry, "People join companies; they leave bosses". Make sure the boss is someone you will actually enjoy working for, even if this means speaking with some of the existing team and also potentially some people who have left (they're easy to find on LinkedIn too, if the employer doesn't offer their details to you).

5. The Team – Who will you be working with on a daily basis and potentially sharing an office with? Are they people you will enjoy spending more of your time with than your actual family (assuming you work full time)? Do you share the same values? Are they people you can imagine having a beer with after work or going to a social event with? Do they have skills and attributes that you admire and which will be synergistic with your own abilities?

6. The Executive Leadership Team – What do you think of the CEO, the Board and/or the company owners? What is their reputation in the market? Another good saying is, "the fish rots from the head down". Do you want to work for a company where the CEO has a reputation for inappropriate behaviour with young female employees, or for making extremely high-risk decisions, for example?

7. The Organisation's Vision and Values – What does the company stand for? Do they want to make the world a better place, or just make as much money as possible? Do they have a clear view of their future goals and strategies to achieve these,

or are they just going with the flow. "When you're green you're growing; when you're ripe you're rotting". Like it or not, you will be judged in the future based on the companies you have worked for in the past.

8. Tools – What tools will you be given to ensure you can do your job to the best of your ability? If you require certain types of technology (specific IT software for example), make sure the company already has it or are prepared to make the investment. If you require a certain budget for travel and marketing expenses to achieve the outcomes required, make sure that it is committed to by the business in advance.

9. Remuneration and Benefits – Are you happy with the salary on offer and any other benefits (vehicle allowance, health insurance, annual leave provisions etc.)? Note that Rem and Ben is only one of eleven factors in this analysis. Don't get too greedy for the highest possible salary, because sometimes when you get paid above your worth, you'll be under the most scrutiny if your own, or the company's performance, is below budget (and therefore you'll be more likely to be made redundant or terminated if you are being paid more than you are actually worth).

10. Work/Life Flexibility – People used to talk about work life balance, however there's an implicit suggestion in this statement that your time at work and not at work must be in balance, or 50/50. For many people they don't actually want this. They love to work hard and do long hours, as long as they can have time off during the day to go to the dentist/manage study requirements etc. Other people only want to work part-time because they have a young family, are a semi-professional

athlete, or have other non-work responsibilities. So I prefer to use the term work/life flexibility, rather than work/life balance.

11. Risk – Is there any perceived risk in taking this job? Could the project be shut down prematurely? Could the role be moved to a different location requiring you to relocate your family or spend long periods away? Is the company potentially going to be sold anytime soon? Of course, every role has some element of risk, and every person has a different level of risk aversion. So you need to assess what is the right degree of risk for you.

Take the time to judge your own current role against these criteria. Really understand why it is you are looking for a new role. Maybe once you do this analysis, you may realise that your current role isn't too bad after all, and that the "problems" you perceive are rectifiable if you speak up and take some responsibility for driving the changes required.

Compare your current role to the other roles you are considering using these criteria. If you are uncertain on some of the elements of roles you are looking at, ask the questions you need to get the clarity required. "To be forewarned is to be forearmed." Don't be shy in asking for whatever information you require to make the best decision you can.

Let's assume you review your current role and make the following conclusions: *"I don't like my boss; he does not acknowledge my achievements and he takes all the credit. The company will not invest in the technology and training I need to keep developing my professional skills. I don't see any future opportunities for promotion beyond my current role. This is why I need to find a new job".* This analysis and self-honesty about your motivations for looking for a new role are very important, as you'll see a bit later in this section.

You have now completed all of the interviews and psychometric testing. The required reference checks have been conducted in order for you to be offered the role. You are the preferred candidate – you are AWESOME. It's time to negotiate the offer.

Firstly, if a recruitment consultant is representing you, there are some things to consider. In the majority of instances the recruiter's fees are a percentage of salary, so the higher the salary they can get you then the more money they will make. The employer though often has a view that the recruiter is being mercenary in their actions, and just trying to talk up the candidate's salary expectations for their own commission benefit. So there is going to be some potential tension here, which you want to ensure is managed well otherwise it could possibly cost you the job.

Also, the recruitment consultant may be working on a contingent basis, meaning they only get paid if you take the job. They may be competing against other recruitment consultants with other candidates. They will be worried that you may price yourself out of consideration, and that they will lose their fee. So in this instance they will try and condition you to take the lowest possible salary. You don't want this either.

(As an aside, high quality recruitment consultants, especially those who work on senior executive roles, should work on a retained basis. This means that they are being paid their fees in instalments over the length of the recruitment process (typically one third at commencement, one third at short list and the balance on acceptance of offer), and they are working exclusively on the role (i.e. not competing with other agencies). Being engaged by the employer on a retained basis means that the recruitment consultant can take a far more professional and unbiased approach to salary negotiations between employer and employee, alleviating the issues raised above.)

Alternatively, you may be dealing directly with the employer and will need to handle the salary negotiations directly with them. This will in some ways change the dynamic of the negotiation process (just like if you were buying a house directly from the owner, versus through a real estate agent), but largely the key elements will remain the same.

The golden rule is that when negotiating salary (or anything based on a quantifiable amount, such as number of weeks annual leave, etc.), then whoever makes the first offer loses!

What I mean by this is that is that the first offer becomes the base line, which the other party will then try and get an advantage from. For example:

Employer (or recruitment consultant): *"What base salary are you looking for in order to accept the role?"*

You: *"$250,000 is my preferred salary."*

Them: *"Look we had only budgeted for $170,000 so are you prepared to accept on that basis?"*

In this example, you'll probably settle on an amount somewhere between $170K and $250K (let's say $205K), which you might be happy with but probably is not the best result for you.

Let's now consider the offer process handled a bit differently:

Employer (or recruitment consultant): *"What base salary are you looking for in order to accept the role?"*

You: *"I would like to be paid what is fair and reasonable for what is required from me to succeed in the role. What would you like to offer?"*

Them: *"We thought $170K would be reasonable."*

You: *"Actually, I had in my mind an expectation of $280K, given what we have discussed about the role so far. I am probably prepared to compromise a little, but $170K is certainly well below my expectations."*

In this example, you'll still end up settling for something between $170K and $280K, but it will probably end up well above the $205K in the above example, which is better for you (assuming you are actually worth it as discussed earlier).

> Very, very rarely does a preferred candidate miss out on a role due to salary, as long as they are not greedy and the salary negotiations are handled properly.

In my experience as an executive recruiter for well over ten years, if the client loves the candidate and the candidate loves the client, then money always works itself out. Very, very rarely does a preferred candidate miss out on a role due to salary, as long as they are not greedy and the salary negotiations are handled properly. This is one of the reasons using a recruitment consultant is beneficial, because they as the negotiator can remove the emotion from the process. However even when negotiating directly with the employer, you can still get a great result. Don't be greedy, whilst still standing your ground and asking for what you want. Your future employer will respect and even value your tenacity, as these are the skills they want in their own executives, especially those in leadership roles.

Once you have finalised your negotiations, you need an employment contract. With a fairly generic role, these can typically be produced quite quickly. With more senior or specialised roles, especially where some unique aspects of the negotiation process have been included, sometimes it takes a while to get an employment contract drafted and then agreed upon. The organisation may need to get their legal counsel to review the document, and you may also want to have a lawyer check the document before you agree to sign it.

NEVER, EVER RESIGN FROM YOUR CURRENT ROLE UNTIL YOU HAVE A SIGNED EMPLOYMENT CONTRACT WITH YOUR NEW EMPLOYER IN PLACE.

Yes, that statement deserves capital letters. My strongest advice is no matter what a company tells you, and even if they give you a written Intent To Offer, nothing is guaranteed until you have a signed employment contract. If something goes wrong (for example you can't agree on a particular condition in the contract, or the document contradicts something you believe you agreed with previously) then the last thing you want to do is be left without a job at all. Even if you are not currently employed, you do not want to close the door on other opportunities until you have a signed employment contract.

Again, your future employer will respect you for being firm in requiring a written contract prior to resigning from your current role. It's the mark of good leadership and good risk management. If they show any resistance to your expectations, then it's probably an early indication that they are not someone you want to work for after all. Time to exit the discussions and find a better alternative.

Once you receive, sign and return your employment contract, you then need to resign from your current role. This is never an easy conversation (unless of course you have a terrible relationship with your boss and will take great delight in resigning). Assuming your relationship is good, it's important to remember that your current boss and employer have made a significant investment in you and that your resignation is going to cause them at least some temporary pain and expense. So be tactful and appreciative for all they have done for you.

Sometimes, your current employer will respond with a counter-offer, because they really need and/or like you, and they don't want you to leave. So they ask what the new job is offering you salary wise, and then they offer to match or exceed the offer for you to stay. Perhaps there are some other conditions they are also prepared to change in order to retain you.

There will be some instances where accepting a counter-offer and staying with your current employer is the right thing to do. Another good saying, "better the devil you know", is a valid reason for staying with your current employer. Perhaps the conditions of the counter-offer are attractive enough that it makes good sense to stay (I once had a situation where a candidate I was representing was on a base salary of $250k. We got him an offer of $350k, which he accepted. He went back to his current employer and resigned, and was counter-offered $450k to stay, which he happily decided to accept. A $200k pay rise in one day – not bad by anyone's standards!).

I recall a statistic I heard some time ago that something like 90 percent of counter-offered candidates, who decide to remain with their current employer, still end up leaving within the next 12 months. I'm not sure how completely true this is, but it's definitely a statistic recruitment consultants will try to tell you if they are fearful of losing their commission. Desperate times call for desperate measures, especially when the recruitment consultant's overseas holiday is on the line!

This is where Lou Adler's eleven-factor analysis is extremely useful. Remember the previous scenario:

> "I don't like my boss; he does not acknowledge my achievements and he takes all the credit. The company will not invest in the technology and training I need to keep developing my professional skills. I don't see any future opportunities for promotion beyond my current role. This is why I need to find a new job".

Let's say your current company offers you an additional pay rise, above what the new employer has offered you, to stay. You need to really think about the fact that money was never your motivation for looking for a new job. You'll still have the same boss, the same lack of training and the same lack of promotional opportunities. Is the offered pay rise enough to compensate for all of that? Maybe it is, but probably it's not.

My greatest advice is to trust your intuition (or for us blokes, trust your gut). In the vast majority of cases, unless you feel completely underpaid in your current role and salary was the main reason for looking for a new job, then don't accept the counter offer. Apart from anything else, your existing boss now has a question mark over your loyalty and will always be wondering when you will next resign. So in most instances remain strong and leave with integrity.

Depending on your contract with your existing employer, you will have a resignation period that you need to adhere to. Sometimes you will be able to negotiate an earlier exit, however this will mean you will need to give up the salary you would have earned during that period, or alternatively not be able to start your new role until the period has expired (this is called "gardening leave").

From a personal integrity perspective, and from a legal standpoint, you need to honour this condition. Likewise if your employment contract contains conditions around restraints of trade, confidentiality, intellectual property etc., my advice is to honour these as well, to the best of your ability. Integrity takes a lifetime to earn, but can be lost in an instant. Even if it seems your future employer may benefit from you breaching some of these conditions, it could also negatively taint their view of you and they may question whether the same thing could happen to them when you eventually leave their employment.

The period between when you resign and when you exit your current company should be the hardest you have ever worked for them. You want to leave with the best impression, because at some point in the future you may need them to be a referee. They could even become a future client or supplier of yours, depending on the work you do. The last thing you want them to think is that you have "dropped the ball" and "put your feet up" post resigning. Ask for complete clarity as to their expectations regarding completing current projects and managing the handover of your responsibilities. Complete every task to the very best of your abilities. Try to leave with friendships intact and without burning any bridges.

In this chapter, I've shown you how to:

- Ensure your referees are going to be excellent advocates for you
- Assess potential opportunities to make sure they are actually what you want and will be the best move for your career
- Negotiate salary offers to achieve the best possible remuneration package for you
- Deal with potential counter-offers from your existing employer and make sure you choose the best outcome for your future career.

CASE STUDY #8:

How Mark, A Communications Manager, Grew His LinkedIn Network By 2000%

Summary:

I had a job in communications, but I was so unhappy in that job. It was going nowhere. There was not room for advancement and I was unhappy with the people I was working for, which was frustrating. I did not want to quit my job until I had another job lined up, so I began to search for another job with a company I would like.

I started looking in 2013 and had already spent nearly a year searching when I found out about the "Always Stand Out" seminar. Actually, my wife heard about the seminar from a talent recruiter and she thought the seminar might help me in my search for a new job. I attended the seminar to find out what I could do to improve my job search results. It was there that I learned essential information on how to grow my LinkedIn network, and I was able to use that information to grow my network significantly in a short period of time. It was through that network that I was introduced to a talent recruiter from the company that is now my employer.

The Problem:

My biggest problem was that I was in a dead end job. I hated going to work, and no one enjoys getting up every morning to head to a hated job. Since I could not afford to quit my job, I started searching for a new job while I was still working. This meant that I did not have a lot of time to put into my job search. I tried using job boards on the web, but most of the time I never even received a response regarding any of the applications I sent in. In that year, I probably applied for about 50 different jobs. I scored one or two interviews but they did not go anywhere.

I did start a LinkedIn profile, but I was not sure how to best set up my profile. I did my best, but I only ended up with a few connections. After several months of using LinkedIn, I still only had 35 connections and none of those connections were helping me as I searched for a job.

Meanwhile, I kept feeling more and more unhappy with the job I was in. I was desperate to find something that would get me out of a job I hated more each day. Since I had spent about a year with no results, I was started to think I was doomed to be stuck in this dead end job for the rest of my life. It was a depressing thought.

The Solution:

My wife has a great job in an unrelated field and one of her friends happens to be a talented recruiter. When her friend found out that I was having a difficult time trying to find a new job, she suggested that I attend the "Always Stand Out" seminar by Richard Triggs. Neither my wife nor I had heard about this seminar or about Richard, but it came highly recommended, so I decided to give it a try. I took a day off work to attend the seminar, hoping that it would give me the tools I needed to finally find a job I really wanted.

That seminar gave me the information I needed to take my LinkedIn profile to the next level. I quickly realised that my profile was atrocious. No wonder I only had 35 connections. My profile was not attracting others and I knew that needed to change. Not only did I learn that my profile needed work, I actually learned how to fix my profile and optimise it so it would generate more profile views, and hopefully, more connections on LinkedIn.

Richard's seminar also touched on finding employers I wanted to work for, as well as how to start reaching out to those employers via LinkedIn messages. I have to admit, the idea of sending out messages to people I wanted to work for seemed scary to me. Selling myself has never been my strong point. I did not think that using messages would work well for me, since I felt uncomfortable doing it.

However, I did like the idea of growing my professional network, so after the seminar I decided to take that course of action. I completely overhauled my LinkedIn profile over several days. I learned more about optimising my profile for search engines so it could be more easily found. I added as much information as possible and worked to ensure that my profile would make people stop and take a second look at me.

I finally felt that I could do something to work towards finding a new job that would help me get out of my current job situation. Just having the hope that this plan might work energised me. I realised that I had a lot to offer and that I needed to communicate that to other people if I wanted a better job.

The Results:

As I used Richard's tips and ideas for optimising my LinkedIn profile, I began seeing results almost immediately. I started receiving connection requests on LinkedIn. My network started to grow quickly. Soon I was up over 100 connections. I was so excited when I topped 200 connections. In two months, I saw 2000% growth in my network – I was up to 700+ connections. I was shocked at how fast I was bringing in good professional connections.

All the new connections helped me start finding potential employers. Those connections have helped me score several interviews as well. One interview in particular went extremely well, and I'm optimistic that I'll be hearing back from the company soon. I believe that my job search is almost over. Even if I learned nothing else but how to optimise my LinkedIn profile, I feel that I definitely benefited from attending the "Always Stand Out" seminar. I learned how to make myself stand out and it's been a significant help to me as I search for an alternative to my current job.

9

SHOWING APPRECIATION TO THOSE WHO HELPED ALONG THE WAY

Hooray – you've now achieved your job of choice with your employer of choice. All the effort in taking control and managing your job search process was worth it. All the emails, phone calls, interview preparation, everything you have invested of yourself into this process has culminated in the best possible outcome – a great new job!

Well done – no wonder you are AWESOME.

Firstly, take the time to appreciate yourself for a job well done. Buy yourself something that you can use every day in your new job, to remind yourself of what a great accomplishment it was in achieving this goal (when I got my last job I bought myself a beautiful leather compendium that I have used every day at work now for the last six years). Maybe take your family on a holiday or do something else special. You deserve it.

Secondly, make sure you also show appreciation to everyone who helped you along the way. Make sure that for everyone who offered advice, was part of the interview process, or acted as a referee, then at the very least tell him or her in person that you got the job and that you are grateful for their assistance.

If a recruitment consultant represented you, this is doubly important, yet so rarely done. Even though I have placed at least a couple of hundred senior executives in my career, I could count on one hand the number of those placed executives that have sent me a bottle of wine (or equivalent) as a thank you. Now before you start feeling sorry for me, don't worry I can afford to provide myself with all the wine I desire (remarkably less than I desired as a younger man!). That's not the point.

The recruitment consultant who placed you no doubt would love some appreciation for the help they have offered you. Sure, they earned a commission, but they still take pride in what they do and a well-intentioned thank you will go a long way. More importantly though, they are out in the market place every day, talking to your peers in the industry, talking to your suppliers, your customers, your thought leaders and your key people of influence. Wouldn't you like them to be talking about you?

I meet with on average about ten CEOs a week. I am regularly asked who are the up and comers within their industries; who are the "movers and shakers" and who to watch out for. These CEOs (and Chairs of boards) are constantly keeping an eye out for the best talent.

One day you will once again be looking for a new role, or maybe you'll be one of those CEOs wanting to have priority access to the best talent in the market. On that basis, perhaps you may want to invest in a long-term relationship with the recruitment consultant who placed you. Even if they didn't place you, it's still in your interest (and theirs) to have a strong and long-term positive influence on each other's careers.

I clearly recall many years ago when a candidate that I secured an offer for, chose to decline it. Even though he said no, he still took the time to send me a thank you card and a bottle of Scotch (I don't drink Scotch but it's the thought that counts). As far as I can recall, it's the only time in my entire recruitment career that anyone sent me a gift for *not* getting them a job!

Do you think I speak favourably about this guy whenever he is brought up in conversation? Do you think I would alert him to other opportunities he may be more attracted to in the future? Absolutely. It goes without saying. In fact, that candidate is now the Chair of a company and they engaged me to recruit their new CEO.

Take the time to thank people that have helped you out. It's common sense and it's an investment in your future.

> Finally, in this chapter you have learned:
> - Everyone who has assisted you in your job search deserves to be recognised and thanked for their assistance
> - Your relationship with the recruiter does not end at placement, and by continuing to invest in this relationship you will open up future opportunities for yourself as an employee and also as an employer.

CONCLUSION

Congratulations on buying this book and making the commitment to read it all the way through. Hopefully you now feel empowered to take control of your own job search, and "Uncover the Hidden Job Market".

> The rise of new technology, in particular LinkedIn, has fundamentally changed the way employers find and hire their staff, and has also allowed job seekers to have unprecedented access to their employers of choice.

We've covered a lot of content, so let's do a quick recap:

The rise of new technology, in particular LinkedIn, has fundamentally changed the way employers find and hire their staff, and has also allowed job seekers to have unprecedented access to their employers of choice. As a job seeker, it is paramount that you have a great understanding of how to use LinkedIn to your advantage, and stand out from the crowd.

In beginning your job search, first you need to decide what you would most like to do next in your career. Would you like the same job in the same industry (just with more preferable conditions, whatever this means for you); would you like to perform the same job in a different industry; or maybe a different job but remaining within your existing industry? Maybe you want a complete change, and desire a new job in a new industry? There are pros and cons in considering any career move, and your job search can't really begin in earnest until you have clearly identified what you actually want your next job to look like.

You are then going to map your chosen market, looking for all potential employers of choice that you can directly approach about opportunities. Firing up your Reticular Activating System, you are going to start compiling lists of employers that you are attracted to.

Once you have listed your individual target employers, you are then going to identify the key person within those organisations that your role will most likely report to. Then you are going to find that person on LinkedIn and send them an introductory message, asking to meet with them for career advice. If they don't have a LinkedIn profile, then you'll call the company and ask for their email address.

Once you've sent your message, then comes the "scary" part. You are going to pick up the phone and call these people, again to ask for a meeting. If they put you off initially, that's ok, you'll just put them into your call cycle for follow up in the future. Remembering this is about achieving your job of choice with your employer of choice, it may take some time to get the job you want.

As well as approaching employers directly to access the hidden job market, you're also going to ensure that when you apply for jobs via advertisements, you develop the best possible relationship with the recruitment consultant to help yourself get prioritised as a preferred candidate. These relationships also take time to nurture and develop, so you will make sure you invest the time necessary to create the best possible engagement with those recruiters who regularly are filling roles in your chosen industry.

Once you get to the initial meeting and subsequent interview stages of a recruitment process, you are going to prepare yourself properly and conduct yourself professionally in order to give the best impression. You're going to ask some killer questions to really help you stand out as an excellent candidate, plus to gather the information you need to ensure you actually want the job on offer.

When offered your perfect role, you're going to negotiate for the best salary package that suits you; and then once you start you are going to ensure you achieve all the early goals and build the best foundation for your future success.

This all sounds so simple, right? And in reality, it actually is simple. There's nothing complicated about any of the information and tools provided in this book. In fact, when you were reading you were probably thinking to yourself, *"This all seems so simple and basic. Why do I need a book to tell me how to do this stuff?"*

However the reality is that, unless you are a truly exceptional job seeker (and I'm yet to meet one), it is most likely you have not been doing all (if any) of the strategies outlined in this book. And if you aren't, you can bet that your competitors (i.e. other job seekers) aren't either. So if you make a commitment to yourself to truly apply the methodologies outlined here, then I guarantee you that you will maximise your ability to achieve your perfect job, quickly and easily.

As I said in the introduction, "the truth is the result", in other words the value of this knowledge is in its application. So please don't put this book down, make yourself a cup of tea, and end up like many of the hundreds of people I have presented this information to over the last few years. Sure, this is a book with some interesting information, and was hopefully a reasonably enjoyable read.

Most importantly, this book is a call to action. Take responsibility for your job search and send the introductory messages and follow up with the phone calls. Set yourself some large activity targets and then make sure you fulfil them. No amount of knowledge is useful unless you put it to good use.

I really look forward to hearing your success stories. All of the people who have implemented the information in this book have gone on to get great jobs and start the next exciting chapter in their careers. I would love it if the next success story was yours.

All the very best in your job search and the next stage in your career.

Richard Triggs

Thanks for buying *Uncover the Hidden Job Market.*

As a reward, I'd like to give you a free copy of my *Always Stand Out* presentation. Simply go to **www.richardtriggs.com/gift**.

You'll also find lots of other useful information and resources.

CPSIA information can be obtained
at www.ICGtesting.com
Printed in the USA
LVHW050422231218
601521LV00019B/679/P

9 780994 218797